T0157493

IT IS TIME

Zeal Akaraiwe

WESTBOW
PRESS®
A DIVISION OF THOMAS NELSON
& ZONDERVAN

Scripture taken from the New King James Version. Copyright © 1979, 1980,
1982 by Thomas Nelson, Inc. Used by permission. All rights reserved.

Scripture taken from the Holy Bible, NEW INTERNATIONAL VERSION®.
Copyright © 1973, 1978, 1984 by Biblica, Inc. All rights reserved worldwide.
Used by permission. NEW INTERNATIONAL VERSION® and NIV® are
registered trademarks of Biblica, Inc. Use of either trademark for the offering
of goods or services requires the prior written consent of Biblica US, Inc.

WestBow Press books may be ordered through booksellers or by contacting:

WestBow Press
A Division of Thomas Nelson & Zondervan
1663 Liberty Drive
Bloomington, IN 47403
www.westbowpress.com
1 (866) 928-1240

Because of the dynamic nature of the Internet, any web addresses or
links contained in this book may have changed since publication and
may no longer be valid. The views expressed in this work are solely those
of the author and do not necessarily reflect the views of the publisher,
and the publisher hereby disclaims any responsibility for them.

Any people depicted in stock imagery provided by Thinkstock are models,
and such images are being used for illustrative purposes only.
Certain stock imagery © Thinkstock.

ISBN: 978-1-5127-0589-8 (sc)
ISBN: 978-1-5127-0588-1 (e)

Library of Congress Control Number: 2015912250

Print information available on the last page.

WestBow Press rev. date: 10/26/2015

CONTENTS

"[1]...Go *your way,* Daniel, for the words *are* closed up and sealed till the time of the end..."

[2]"...Now when the seven thunders uttered their voices, I was about to write; but I heard a voice from heaven saying to me, "Seal up the things which the seven thunders uttered, and do not write them..."

---

[1] Daniel 12:9 NKJV
[2] Revelation10:4 NKJV

There are those days you wake up on the right side of bed with an uplifting song in your heart and everything about life and nature is simply beautiful. You step out of the house knowing you're looking dapper in your brand new tailored cashmere blazer made from the finest Mongolian mountain goats, spun in Ireland and tailored in Italy. Sunrise is nothing but perfect as the sun's mild morning rays travel down into the earth's atmosphere uninhibited by cloud lines. As I drove from the house, it was quite a surprise that for a bustling city, there was absolutely no traffic and at the same time, all traffic lights were green for at least the last 6 stops. In the background was the amazingly soothing, crystal clear melody of "6 WORDS" by Wretch 32 booming from the B&O surround system of my brand new Audi A5 custom convertible - this must surely be the life dreams are made of and just as I veered left to turn into my office street, in an instant the car seemed to be driving itself because I could swear I was turning left not right. The sound of crunching metal brought home reality as I bizarrely found myself facing oncoming traffic. My perfect morning world was inexplicably brought to an abrupt end.

In the recent past, I've read a good share of self help and mind control books and always prided myself on the fact that I can remain calm through practically any conceivable storm. I just hadn't had my car knocked off the road for no reason before and so my definition of "conceivable storm" was somewhat limited in that regard. All those calming mantras seem to have succumbed to my temporary amnesia as whatever lobe in my brain they were stored found wings and escaped through my ears. The only words I seemed to find were those I didn't even know existed in my vocabulary. Amazingly, I was able to hold a good measure of some of those words back as I shouted in the direction of the car that had knocked me sideways. "What on earth were you looking at? Didn't you see your light was red? Did only half of your brain develop through childhood?"

"Oga, please remain calm," the driver replied as he stepped out of his car. Is he for real, I wonder? Remain calm? It's not easy to keep any type of calm, in fact, that word has a totally different definition right now. I bring out my phone to call the Police whilst the driver, expectedly, pleads and cries. His pleas seem to only succeed in infuriating me the more and though I do not have a violent streak in me, there was this urge to …….I'm not allowed to say what I really felt like doing.

Suddenly a distinguished man stepped out from the pitch black interior of the tinted car with an aura I cannot explain. It wasn't arrogance – confidence, yes, but a kind that you could almost feel and taste. I had only just noticed that the car was a snow white 2010 Bentley with a customised plate number which read, "No Time". That kind of explains things. With a license plate like that, of course you'd always be in a hurry while causing problems for everyone else. But as time would tell, the license plate had a whole different meaning from my initial interpretation.

He also tried to calm me down and then asked if I really felt it was absolutely necessary to get the Police involved, to which I quickly retorted, "Justice must be done." I have an exceptionally quick tongue and normally, good wit for a small frame like mine. I'm well known for having an answer to everything but his next question, "What would you call justice?" kinda caught me off guard. Just what I needed this morning – an "over-smart" old man that, given my upbringing, I can't be rude to. "Well, Justice is that my car gets fixed and the driver gets punished."

"What type of insurance do you have? With a flashy car like this, comprehensive I'd presume." Aha, I knew where he was going with this line of thought and all the wheels and pulleys in my brain were spinning really fast.

"So", he continued, "your car will get fixed and I assure you, I shall punish the driver, so justice, as defined by you, is done, right?" I felt like I had simultaneously engaged the swallowing of horse tranquiliser with the ice bucket challenge. What is it about this man that's so enchanting and disarming and yet sends chills down my spine? It wasn't so much what he said as it was the way it sounded in my ears. His tone was firm and authoritative and the look in his eyes was piercing and yet distant all at the same time. I couldn't tell if he was looking at me, through me or into me – in all honesty, it seemed like he was doing all three.

"Yes, of course it's comprehensive." My vocal chords decided to return to normal pitch after squealing like a trapped rat. "I guess so." He smiled a broad smile, which seemed to display a look that was more pity than amusement. "Here's my card", he said, "call me." Then he turned around entered his car with his driver and they drove off. They left. Just like that, he actually left me standing in the middle of the road holding in my hands a worthless card in place of my ego. I finally did a proper examination of the damage to my car to figure out if I could still drive it away or if I needed to get it towed. It was odd, quite odd - my car was barely scratched. It dawned on me, quite embarrassingly, how silly I must have looked throwing such a tantrum.

3months had passed since my awkward encounter with that old man and 3months since I wore that amazing blazer and 3months since I received the very weird card from him. In my rage I had just stuffed the card into my jacket pocket and I never even took a look at it until now. In front, all it had was "Pa Abraham" and a phone number. It also had a rather beautiful crest behind. The 3D crest was embossed and the best description I can give is that it's like silver and gold embroidery carved unto dark wood, but since this was a paper card I'd just say it had an extremely unique and surreal look. What a laugh though. Where I'm from, this is what "419s" are made of – an elaborate complimentary card without an address or even a full name, just a presumably real first name and a phone number. Nonetheless, after a few hours of attempting to resist the urge to call, my curiosity got the better of me. Maybe I wasn't paying attention, maybe I was even daydreaming while I dialed, maybe it was the usual network issues we have grown accustomed to, but I swear with my entire being, the phone didn't ring before "Pa Abraham" picked up and promptly said "My dear Son, you finally called, I've been waiting." "H-H-How didididididid you know it was me" – what's' wrong with me around this man? When did I start to stutter?

"I'm having breakfast tomorrow at The Cuisine. Join me at 9 am, don't be late," and he hung up. Seriously? Apart from my ex, I have not met anyone who could, like a pendulum, swing my emotions from one extreme to the other in such a short time. And that's EXACTLY why she's an ex. I was irritated, intrigued, impressed, confused and upset all at the same time. He must think I have nothing better to do with my time tomorrow than to get up on a weekday and indulge in breakfast at 9 am, not even 7 am or 7.30 am. Or perhaps I look retired and jobless like he does. He must not know how hard I worked and he must think I have a slush fund somewhere that was handed to me.

After all the ranting and deliberation within myself, I still woke up the next day, earlier than normal, excited that I was going to see him that morning. Frankly, I barely slept through the night.

It's amazing the little twists of fortune or otherwise that life throws in to alter your entire existence. With that singular car accident, with that new blazer that didn't routinely go to the drycleaners with everything else, with that overdue phone call, with that breakfast, a new world was opened up to me. A world of intrigue, wisdom and experience. A world of the supernatural. A simple world of what I call "reverting paradigm shift", if that makes any sense.

BREAKFAST

I was about 4 minutes late and quite unlike me too. I know it was 4 minutes because there's this radio program I usually listen to at 9 am whenever I'm in the car at that time and I was sad that on this day, I'd miss it. It had just about started when I pulled into the street and I reckoned it was about a 3-minute drive to the building from the gate and perhaps another minute or so for parking. Yes, I'm weird like that with timing. Honestly, I didn't expect Pa Abraham to be there at precisely 9 am. First, he looked 70, even though rather good looking for 70, assuming he was really 70 and not closer to 90 like I suspected. Why would he be up and about so early? Besides, in this town of mine, no one really keeps to time.

It was rather easy spotting him from way across the room, sitting next to the only large window close to the single lampshade that threw a subtle ambient light on the Pierre-Auguste Renoir 1886 painting on the wall.

"Goodmo….." – He didn't let me finish before he cut me off with a very abrupt "So, why are you still single?" I couldn't believe the cheek of him, but I was quite ready for him this time around. I had tossed and turned all night and anyone who saw me would think I was nervous over a pending job interview or a first date with a stunning model. Did I mention I had stayed awake till 3 am rehearsing every possible permutation and combination of questions he might have – except this!

Nonetheless, I was quite ready for this game of questions that I am quite familiar with, except that I am usually the one on the giving not receiving end of this kind of banter.

"Why do you think that I am not married?"

"I did not say you are not married, I asked why you were single – even though I now also know you aren't married." I will confess, he had a very good-natured brusqueness, if there's any such thing; curt, but just shy of rude. Something about his expression came across as good-natured so it was hard to read his words as anything but.

"Well", I started, "I am married. I have a wife and 2 kids. I got married 3 years ago." I'm still not certain why I felt the urge to lie about that, I just didn't want him to be right.

He laughed. "No, you most certainly are not. First, you said you have a wife, which lays undue emphasis on her existence and role, which means you want me to believe she exists because she doesn't. I didn't ask about your kids yet you generously volunteered the information when you should ordinarily and instinctively be protecting the truth from a stranger; and then you said you've been married 3 years because most probably that's when you ideally should have been or when you had a plan to get married. So, your answer is much more likely the plan you fantasise about but not reality."

Listen for people who answer the questions you didn't ask, for in those answers lie the deception – a principle I live by and even teach and yet, I've just been caught out on it. The truth is very often right in your face if only you can exercise the discipline to listen to all that is not being said and weigh the details against the circumstance.

Quick emotion check! Disarmed? Absolutely! Feeling silly? Check!

"So how did you know I was single?"

"I didn't but when my driver and I ran into you 3 months ago, the speed at which you jumped out of the car without looking at yours, especially without looking at yours, and came straight at my driver suggested to me that you haven't been through the torturous school of balancing and prioritising and of consequence! Marriage usually teaches you that very quickly. I suspected then and so I asked now."

In all of 10 minutes and before the breakfast order was taken, I very quickly realised that I had unnecessarily deprived myself of sleep. There are some battles you can only win by not fighting. I sensed a deep well of wisdom in Pa Abraham and decided that instead of resisting, instead of showing I could be as good, instead of my usual wit for wit responses, I would simply yield and tap into his well. After all, what did I have to prove to the old man?

The familiar smile indicated that the waiter knew Pa Abraham very well. More intriguing though, was that Pa Abraham knew, in my opinion, what I would consider insignificant details about this waiter's personal life.

"How's your son doing now Peter? Hope he has stopped limping and is back to playing soccer?"

"He's great sir, the therapy you suggested worked like magic. English breakfast, warm water and honey with a slice of freshly cut lime, home-made marmalade and a bottle of lukewarm water as always sir?"

I could also read a lot from the breakfast order and it told me quite a bit about Pa Abraham's attitude. The order is very specific and the waiter actually remembers. Pa Abraham is health conscious, meticulous and pedantic without the fussiness and attitude associated with people of that sort. He's obviously a caring man with an extra dose of humility. What we call a nice easy-go-lucky guy.

The waiter glanced at me and I nodded in agreement with Pa Abraham's order. I figured I'd just have the same thing.

"So how did you know I was the one calling?" a question that had been gnawing away at me all night.

"Why did it take you so long to call?"

"Why are you answering a question with a question?"

"You tell me, you just did it as well."

Our breakfast was awesome. We spoke mostly about life: the after-life, pre-life and the things that make up life especially the correlation between spiritual well-being and religion. I noticed though, that Pa Abraham had a distinct discomfort discussing "religion" as I understood it. He preferred to discuss worship and serving the Almighty outside of the context of religion. He spoke a lot about many ancient writings in very many books and I marvelled at how his memory was so crisp for such an old man.

"You have quite some depth in the Bible and its teachings, but I noticed you never refer to the Bible as anything other than one of the "Holy Books". You also seem to not be too familiar with the details in it, but you are extremely knowledgeable about the principles. Do I take it you aren't a Christian?"

"Well, that really depends my son, on who you refer to as a Christian. Are you asking if I go to a church at least once a week and more likely on a Sunday than any other day? If that's what you mean, then no, I am not a Christian.

"If however, you are asking if I teach and practice the principles of loving the Almighty God, the Creator of the Universe and if I love and help all those I can; if you are asking if my heart is pure towards the things the Creator loves and if I live a life without erring from His commandments written in my heart, then yes, I am a Christian.

"So, which are you referring to?

"I'm sure you will agree that not everyone that goes to church on Sundays or any other day is a Christian. We are certainly both agreed on that point. I actually believe that most of those in church on Sunday aren't even Christians at all, in the true sense.

"So, if going to church doesn't make you a Christian in the sense you mean, then it must also follow that not everyone who doesn't go to church isn't a Christian."

Aha, I sensed a trap again. And I distinctly remembered the lesson on "when you have nothing to say, say nothing". And so I kept mute and waited.

"I certainly believe in God Almighty, the one and only true God. I just don't agree that His plan for mankind is for us to confine Him to some building or the other, or some day of the week or make images of Him and call on Him in specific places. I don't believe that the worship of Him takes place anywhere other than in our hearts and thus exudes daily in our words and deeds.

To be honest, I barely go to church because I do not believe in the many self-proclaimed "MEN OF GOD" and "PASTORS" and whatever else they call themselves these days who simply prey on the innocence and laziness of many people and pretend to act as a bridge that they aren't.

"I do love the company of like minds when it comes to the worship and service of the Almighty and I have found so many people that, in my opinion, worship him truly but would certainly be shunned by your so-called "Christians".

"Mahatma Gandhi is someone whose company was great. He understood the principles of the Creator deeply and he came across like he did his best to follow them with all his heart. He read about Christianity and realised that its core principles were the same as those that were handed to him and so one day, he decided to go to church. Having read the Bible a bit and finding that the teachings of Jesus were totally and completely true, he figured that church, the place where the teachings of Jesus should be studied and practiced, would be a gathering of like minds and like hearts. He figured he would be able to not only share, but also learn from a much deeper pool than he could imagine. He was so excited heading towards the church that day.

"The reason he never returned to church is the same reason I do not attend. Despite the great proliferation of the church in our world today, the weed has surely outgrown the garden; the decayed is by far more than the preserved; the corruption around in the world today tells me that the "salt" truly has lost is potency to preserve, so of what use then is it?"

I had to interject here, "Isn't that a bit generalist and a rather harsh summary of a group of people, of which some are certainly doing God's work? And I really don't think it's in our place to judge. After all, the "Holy Book" you have referred to says judge not and also says touch not my anointed."

"Well young man, perhaps I am lumping both good and bad but I offer no apology. As for your quotes, you, along with so many others I have come across in this journey of mine, often quote scripture either incompletely or out of context, without thought, with very little understanding and even less intellect.

"You pick and choose verses from the various Holy Books based on what seems right and convenient in your own eyes and for the immediate situation and then you project it to either intimidate or create guilt. If ever there were an abuse so dire, it would be what I have seen by those who twist the words of the Prophets and the Lord in his books in order to achieve a self-fulfilling end. I have seen so-called men of God in so many so-called religions hold holy books in all sobriety and sincerity and lead many people astray. For many years, I have seen and observed young and old men and women, raise their hands, bow their heads, pray fervently, sit under the tutelage of people handed the Spirit for the purpose of reconciling mankind to God. I have seen these men due to distractions, high handedness, misunderstandings, arrogance, self confidence, complacency, greed and selfish financial and political interests twist and distort and quote the Word out of context and deceive many.

"I meet so many people who merely read the Holy Books and yet, we are asked to STUDY and MEDITATE on them, not just read. I could read a novel, I could even read literature for an exam; but you certainly don't "read" Math nor Physics – you study them – pen, paper, notes, questions, tests and so on. The Holy Books are to be studied my son, not read; after all, it does say "Study to show thyself approved unto God", doesn't it?"

Wow, Pa Abraham was clearly agitated. I could see the veins on his neck and forehead popping. This was clearly a topic of passion for him and I was somewhat intimidated. The pain he experienced from talking about this could be felt. Even I, sitting across from him and not even part of the people he was referring to felt a sense of guilt for no conceivable reason. But still, I didn't like the fact that he seemed not to care that there were sincere men of God out there and I didn't want to back down. So I decided to prod a little more.

"Why would you say such a harsh thing? Don't you think that you are guilty of that which you accuse others?"

He smiled. A tender amused smile. He seemed to have calmed down. Then he asked me, "Let me go back to your earlier comment: who in your own understanding and scriptural context is referred to as the anointed?"

"Well," I began to stutter again, "must be the pastors and the men of God that He has called to do His work."

"Well," Pa Abraham started, "you are not correct in that specific context. In the context you speak, everyone who has a calling from God would be His anointed. That particular scripture which is (mis)quoted by many to give room to erring servants of the Almighty to do ill without reproach, refers to the days where prophets and kings were called by the Almighty Himself either directly or through covenants tied to lineage or through other prophets. In those days, the High Priest would carry out a ceremony where oil is poured over the head of he that had been called. The oil is anointing oil and the person becomes "the anointed one". In our own time, you can jolly well start a group tomorrow and declare yourself anointed and everyone would senselessly follow you and whatever teaching you share. I laugh at the herd of humans I see who forget that the stuff they have in-between their ears was put there for a good reason.

"On the other issue you raised about judging, let me ask, if I blindfolded you and took you to a tree and asked you to pluck its fruit and taste and by the feel, shape and taste of the fruit, you discern that it's an apple tree and you therefore declare that I took you to an apple tree; are you judging?

What if, just for argument's sake, the apple tree tells you it is an orange tree and that you are being judgmental by calling him an apple tree? What if he brings ten other trees to confirm that right from when he was a seedling they knew him and raised him as an orange tree? And what if ten other passersby agree and confirm it is an orange tree and then turn around and accuse you that you have jumped to conclusions based on too little evidence since you had only tasted a single fruit. Would all that change your assessment?"

"Come on, Pa Abe, of course that's a totally different scenario. If it's an apple tree then that's what it is. It has nothing to do with what he thinks. He is what he is and if he doesn't know what he is, then perhaps he is the one with the problem and not me. And if all those people decide to nurture and believe a lie, I certainly will not follow suit. They can check and test for themselves, can't they?"

"That's my point my son, if I see a man call himself something and yet, he sounds like, behaves like and bears the fruit of something else, how am I judging by calling him what he really is? You see, in my years I have traveled far and wide and crisscrossed all continents, visiting at least 70 countries and had deep discussions spanning 14 religions. I've met a lot of these self proclaimed men of God but from their fruit, by their nature, by their desires, they are children of the Devil himself. Never mind that in front of their followers they have the gait of piety and speak as though the words from their mouths are sacred and from a trance. Not so deep inside, they are pompous and greedy and proud and unkind and love money much more than God and yet, I am told not to judge? I am not judging my son, I am simply describing the tree by the fruit. Doesn't the Holy Book say [3]"you shall know them by their fruits"?"

"Well, as for me sir, I am not used to nor comfortable speaking against people in authority and this conversation is very awkward. You are making a lot of sense but I just can't bring myself to agree. Frankly, I'd rather just ignore them and leave them to God and their conscience to judge. After all, how do I know what's going on in their hearts."

Pa Abraham looked me straight in the eye and once again, it was impossible to tell if he was looking at me, through me or into me. It was a

---

[3] Matthew 7:16

terribly uncomfortable type of gaze that leaves you feeling exposed and vulnerable. It did feel as though he was searching my heart. Though the look lasted just a split second it felt like an eternity and then I saw in his eyes, a combination of what seemed to be pity and pain and I was suddenly filled with a great sense of guilt.

"Yes, I hear that a lot. That's the lazy and cowardly way out. By encouraging that line of thinking, "they" have enslaved and indoctrinated their followers so they do not ask questions, and then they lead them like sheep to the slaughter; sheep who should know better and perceive truth but follow because they don't want to be the odd one out.

"Look son, it's up to everyone and their belief system and I will ordinarily not come between a man and his belief. However, my concern comes from the ripple effect it is creating in society."

"What are you talking about sir?"

"You said you aren't used to speaking against people in authority and you'd rather leave them to their conscience. Well, look around you and see the leaders you have in your country! They do not have any conscience and no one speaks against them. So what happens? You have been trained to be complacent and idiotic by the very institution that should empower you and embolden you to be firm and just. The same institution that should teach you reason and justice deadens your spirit and senses to these same things and yet, you can't see how wrong it is.

"I'm sure you've heard the maxim "vox populi vox dei" – whether or not I believe it is a discussion we can have at another time but here, when I look around I see that the "populi" really have no "vox" and therefore you have thrown "Dei's vox" out of the equation. But at the same time, we claim that everything that has happened is from Him.

"It's like a man coming into your house holding a Holy Book and after stealing all that you have, raping your family, killing those who resisted, turns around and tells you that because God is all powerful and because He is all knowing, if He allowed him to succeed in robbing you, raping you and destroying your life then it is the will of God. This man also turns around and convinces you using the Holy Book that you are being judgmental if you call him a thief and a murderer. And you, my dear friend, very stupidly agree.

"Your generation is breeding people whose culture excludes the questioning of authority, who will not challenge immorality at the top, who have grown accustomed to turning a blind eye, who believe that being taken for granted is a privilege – you are breeding a perverse generation that will bring you sudden and certain destruction. Instead of training your minds and standing for what you should, you leave it to the conscience of the people who have usurped authority, and then you call on the Almighty to save you in the time when you are reaping what you have so meticulously and painstakingly sown. No my son, it doesn't work that way. If your generation continues on this path of sowing timidity and watering it with deceit and then throwing in recklessness as fertiliser, while tolerating the weeds of complacency, you will with all certainty, reap disaster.

"Let me help you piece some things together that I am sure are pretty apparent and you are quite aware of but have terribly ignored.

"We know that culture is a way of life of a people and we also know that culture isn't static – it evolves. What culture was 100 or 200 years ago may or may not still be practiced exactly as it was before. I remember a country I visited many years ago that had a culture of putting out water for their guests to wash their feet before entering the house. I found it hilarious, but it made sense considering it was arid land, sandals seemed to be the only footwear they had and trekking was the major means of mobility. With civilisation came some shoes, as did socks and tarred roads with cars and of course, much less dirty feet. They tried really hard to hold on the tradition, but the new generation laughed it to extinction.

"Now think about your country and all the citizens that are below 18 today, matter of fact, I'd even dare say 25. What culture are they imbibing? What is the predominant way of life that they are accustomed to? What are the things they consider normal? To what psychological evolutionary process are they exposed?

"Let me paint a picture for you: many would never, in their entire lives, have driven on properly tarred roads and few understand what having power for 24 hours at a stretch is (perhaps they don't even know what having power 24 hours a week is). They believe that security forces can neither protect them nor solve crime; they only see and hear of political office holders in the context of corruption and not performance; they see elections as a process to take power and they have never heard of a political office holder being accountable to the people and they probably don't know the difference between a bribe, gift and extortion. From where they sit, good education is prohibitively expensive and only for the very few affluent who can afford it.

"I'll stop here, but I hope you get the picture. Human nature is designed largely, to revert to what it considers "normal" and whenever anything or anyone attempts to bring about change, the first thing you will notice is resistance because we are too fearful of the unknown. Everyone wants to revert to what they consider normal. So, when injustice becomes normal, when bribery becomes normal, when lack of accountability becomes normal, when theft by politicians and public officials becomes normal, when bad roads become normal, when failure of the educational, health and security systems become normal; when we make the ills of society normal and the young ones get used to it, what do you think happens when the children grow and become decision makers? Naturally, they will resist change. Naturally they will always want to revert to what they consider normalcy. They will fight to the death to ensure that status quo is maintained. They will begin to destroy and demolish and tear down anything that they consider abnormal – and in the future, at this rate, all good things will become abnormal.

"They will rationalise and make laws that will punish you for being abnormal – like if you don't steal enough. Of course, what we call stealing has taken on a definition that defies any reasonable logic.

"Like Dresden James said ***"when a well-packed web of lies has been sold gradually to the masses over generations, the truth will seem utterly preposterous and its speaker a raving lunatic"***.

"Allow me to digress to illustrate that point.

"I once had a long discussion with a man in his 60s who held that inflating contracts was profit and that it was neither stealing nor corruption and his logic went thus: "if you were a trader of any kind, at what point would your profit margin move from "profit" to "stealing" or "corruption"? After all, a contract awarded by the government with a 10% mark up would be fine; perhaps 20% as well and as long as there's no law stating an acceptable stipulated mark up, then whatever you can get away with is fine. If the government thought it too high, they shouldn't give the contract.

"Although I could punch all sorts of holes in that argument, it was the sincerity of his conviction that I couldn't help but be amazed by. He truly believed himself. That my son, is a sad and dangerous trend.

"I used to believe that nation building and religion should be kept as far apart as possible. I believed the perception that politics is an extremely dirty game and is only ever full of deception and the use of people to achieve a personal goal.

"I have, over the years, come to accept that the question isn't whether or not politics and religion should be intermingled, but to what extent and in what manner they must be. I will accept that this is a terribly slippery slope to tread, an amalgamation that is more open to abuse and manipulation than any other, but then, it is therefore one that must be skillfully and diligently undertaken.

"The tenets of many legal systems and the constitutions of many countries are built with the same fibres on which the foundations of many religions are structured; fairness, equity, civil living, peaceful dispute resolution, reward for good action and punishment of bad."

Now, the next few chapters describe the lessons I learnt from Pa Abraham over many more breakfast meetings.

He instructed that I share them for as he said, the existence of mankind and our ability to attain spiritual paradise, depends on it.

SHOULD I REASON?

One of the hardest and obviously counterintuitive things to do, is to apply reason while teaching or learning anything to do with religion (from time to time, I shall interchange the word "religion" with "faith"). But I refer, not to the faith that's required to worship and honour and follow the ordinances of an unseen Creator, I refer to the faith that is demanded of us by men who ask us to believe that the words and ordinances they spew from their mouths are indeed the mind and commandments of the Creator. I refer to the faith misconstrued to be blind followership demanded by many self-proclaimed "men of God". It deadens your senses, removes your reasoning and entices you with pleasing the Creator by obeying, **without question**, their own selfish commands and sometimes misinterpretations of the words in the Holy Books.

A lot of worshippers today are not applying any form of reasoning to the faith they profess and they believe that this is the type of faith demanded by God. It is NOT! This type of blind, unthinking followership is worship of the messenger in the worst cases and emotional sentiment in the least!

We have heard of self proclaimed "men of God" who have asked members to drink poison or petrol, or eat grass or even those who have asked young men and women to strap explosives to themselves and kill as many as they can.

Let me attempt to use a story to illustrate how some of us look when we simply take in the words of others without testing or proving them:

"A powerful man once had a son in his very old age that he was extremely fond of and because they were generations apart, communication wasn't as smooth as it ought to be. Since the son was granted unlimited access to his father, the son made it a point of duty to speak with his father daily to seek wise counsel and share experiences. One day, some men met the lad in the field and told him that they were his father's messengers and that his father had sent them to tell him to travel to a far country and bring

him gifts of rare robes and precious stones. They told the son that the father wanted him to go on the journey as quickly as possible and they even hinted that a test of his son-ship was his immediate obedience. The lad contemplated for a while and wondered why his father, whom he had spoken with daily, had not told him of his plan to send him away on such a journey. He wondered what the unexpected urgency was and why his father felt the need to suddenly test his so-called son-ship. Of course, the messengers pressed on him that the journey had to be taken immediately and that any delay could cause unnecessary harm to their relationship. The lad then, after deep contemplation, insisted on going back to confirm with his father what the messengers had said. Of course, they had some evidence of having been in contact with his father, but these were not messengers that his father had used in the past to communicate with him and neither were they introduced by his father. These were messengers who merely claimed to be messengers.

What do you think a wise and thoughtful son should do in cases like these? But again, only a son who has regular and unimpeded access to his father would have the boldness to go back to him. Only a son with the confidence that his father will entertain his presence and speak back would even dare go and crosscheck. Only a son with a clear conscience would understand that his father will willingly disclose his hearts' desires.

It is the same with the Almighty Father of all…….not some!

However, on the other hand, if this is the state of mind of a son who would go back, then what type of son wouldn't? What type of son would prefer, for fear of offending his father, to listen to the strange words of strangers? What son would tell you, "if they are wrong or lying, I'll leave judgment to my father?" Or "better safe than sorry."

Now if the messengers were well known to the son and the father sent them with messages to him regularly, in the course of their daily interactions, the son would know his father's intents and plans for him and would easily follow the messages that are in line with his father's intent. When those messages drift from what the son knows to be his father's intent, he would wait till he sees or speaks with his father to get a better understanding of why he is shifting from his original intent. It may well be that the messengers misunderstood the message, misdirected it, or even plainly made it up.

If for any reason after the father has shared his intent with his son, and a messenger gives the son instructions which contradict his father's intent; if the son follows such a message, the father would be a lot more cross with the son than with the messenger. I imagine such a son would qualify to be called foolish!

"[4]And a stranger will they not follow, but will flee from him: for they know not the voice of strangers...."

Of course, all this is on the very basic assumption that there is actually a relationship between the son and the father. If this relationship doesn't exist, then there can only be chaos, confusion, misdirection and deception. This will give ample room for the false prophets who are described as [5]ferocious wolves in sheep's clothing, disguised as part of the flock but their sole intent and aim is to [6]exploit the sheep.

---

[4] John 10:5
[5] Matthew 7:15 (NIV)
[6] 2Peter 2:3

It is important therefore to have both a channel of communication with the Creator and a filter to what you hear. That filter is reason.

The Creator put something between your ears for a very good and specific reason – to apply reason. Even where He is concerned, keeping your reasoning abilities intact is absolutely necessary even if it is just to make a decision to debunk the need to apply conventional reasoning. Either way, you must make a conscious decision and not an emotional one. After all, faith cannot be credited to you unless you have the choice not to have it; and that choice can only possibly come from reason. Faith is in fact, choosing to believe in spite of overwhelming physical evidence that you shouldn't. Faith is deciding against the odds – it is not "not deciding", and deciding always involves a thought process.

When Abraham was asked to sacrifice his son, he applied a faith that not many people today can even begin to understand not to mention replicate; but he also applied reason. Contradictory as it may sound, his wasn't an unthinking faith. It was a firm belief in the ability of the Almighty to do the impossible – processed in his brain and carried out by his spirit. The Holy Book does state that

Abraham applied reasoning before attempting to sacrifice his son. It was reasoning that led him to the faith. It was an understanding of God's power, a calling to remembrance of God's promise (of a son) and then a submission to that power to fulfill the promise one way or the other. "[7]Abraham **reasoned** that God could raise his son from the dead".

When you reason, it becomes clearer what exactly you believe and the choice you make to believe it becomes a lot stronger and more compelling. You make a conscious choice to debunk reasoning. Many of the things I believe about religion, I have come to realise were simply shoved down my throat with a threat of being branded as an "unbeliever". Even more than that, I have come to the stern realisation that a lot of what I thought I knew or believed were baseless and some of them, even inaccurate. I therefore learnt to study for myself and read (in context). The Encyclopedia became my ally and when I found Google, I was in ecstasy. A lot of the things I "knew" started to crumble, a lot of my "beliefs" when tested, began to fail. I saw that I had been on a very long journey along a path that mostly

---

[7] Hebrews 11:19 (NIV)

didn't exist. I found that with my faith and with my belief system, I was on an imaginary road leading nowhere, at best.

Sometimes you don't know what you believe till you have to believe what you know.

Now though, I've been doing a lot of reasoning when it comes to religion and there are many things I still choose to believe with a few that I have accepted are irrelevant and neither here nor there. But, there are these few things that, even though my belief hasn't changed, my understanding has. I am a million times better, my knowledge is razor sharp and my decision making, precise.

I have seen many a clash between science and religion; specifically, the science around the creation of the universe. I often smile and wonder when I listen to the heated debates around the "big bang" and probable life on other planets and all that. To me it is a rather simple issue - religion tells me exactly what the Creator did. Now, it is the emotional faith that, without reasoning, debunks all of the scientific theories without even considering because of a blind and uncompromising state of mind. Personally, I do not see why both cannot co-exist and be equally accurate. Religion tells me WHAT the Creator did and science attempts to tell me HOW.

You see, the lucky ones actually choose what to believe. (There are some people who by virtue of the geographical location of their birth, their parents' disposition or the specific historical period they were born, had beliefs instilled in them and they never had the opportunity to choose. Frankly, most humans, in the matter of religion, didn't have a choice – they followed their parents.) Now, that belief, however it was formed, is based on a mindset and there's very little you can do to change it. The person has to, within himself, decide to seek a reason to hold on or change. Therefore, that decision requires, generally, a paradigm shift.

ABRAHAM APPLIED REASON

I studied one of the Holy Books and realised that I could summarise the entire book as the story of a single man. I studied this man's life and found many of the things I thought I knew about him weren't actually true, or rather, weren't based on anything other than my childhood imagination and recollection of non-existent facts.

First, I always imagined that the Almighty spoke to this man the same way I imagine He speaks to some people today – in their heads or in dreams, and perhaps with signs or with a voice from above.

After re-reading his story, I came to the realisation that the Almighty spoke to him as I speak to my friends today – as a walking, talking man. When the Almighty called him a friend, He meant EXACTLY that: a friend. They sometimes sat together and shook hands and hugged and ate and talked and walked. They were your regular buddies.

Christians and Jews know The Almighty as JEHOVAH or JAH or Yahweh or I AM THAT I AM (though when you study its translation from the Hebrew, it's *Ehyeh-Asher-Ehyeh* - a much deeper meaning than "I Am That I Am" – "I will be whatever I will be" – meaning God is both self sufficient and self defining). It could also mean "I am who I shall be", illustrating a constancy irrespective of perceived variations.

If you think about it, these all happen to be His names and much more specifically, His names in the Hebrew language. Indeed Abraham and his descendants through Jacob are all Hebrew and I doubt that the Almighty would have introduced Himself in a language other than theirs.

Considering Abraham could probably speak only one language, it would have been abundantly hilarious for God to hold discussions with Abraham in French or Yoruba.

I truly don't imagine that He would have met a French man on the street as He did Saul and introduced Himself in Japanese. It must be understood and appreciated that practically all you know about The Almighty is from the Hebrew perspective and I imagine that accepting Him from any other perspective would indeed be difficult but it should not be entirely disregarded.

I often wonder if God truly revealed Himself to only one man in the whole of the earth as He did to Abraham. I've asked myself what the possibility was that God also had a friend like him in some other part of the earth like in India, China or somewhere in Africa. I've wondered if there are also records kept of such friendships and how the modern religious world would react if we came across such accounts.

Abraham was God's close friend and a record of that is kept and you have access to that record and that is, simply put, the only reason you have that choice of that faith. Now, just imagine that God also had friends in Asia and Africa and South America – do you think they would call Him Jehovah? Certainly not!! Before the missionaries traveled far and wide and introduced the Bible (which had the names of God I have mentioned), was God not worshipped? Was He not called upon? I firmly believe that He would have introduced Himself to various cultures in their own language and guess what – perhaps a record of that friendship is kept in a "book" and we either have no access to it, or even if we do, we are too prejudiced to read it.

We need to understand that the Almighty revealed Himself to quite a few people and I am sure not all encounters are recorded in the Bible or Koran – I am relatively certain that there is no one book that has all the encounters recorded. So for example, if we consider Job – was he an Israelite? – I can almost certainly say no. But the record is clear that he worshiped the true God, and that God loved him and was so proud of him that He actually showed him off in Heaven. It is clear that God spoke to him, commanded him, watched over him and it is clear he worshipped God truly. The same goes for Noah. Was he an Israelite? Certainly not - for Israel was not yet born in his time. God was upset with the inhabitants of the earth and resolved to wipe them out. But He saved Noah and his household, why? It is on record that Noah was a righteous man; he walked with God and was blameless. Even the prophet Balaam was certainly not a Jew and yet he was well known as a prophet that God spoke to. When Balak the King of Moab called him to curse the Israelites, he enquired from God whether or not to go and God responded to him. There's no single record of any of the prophecies and divinations done by Balaam to have given him the highly esteemed reputation he had, except the one incident that brought him in direct confrontation with the children of Abraham. If not for that, he would probably have remained completely unknown (from the point of view of the Bible). Can you begin to imagine how many more must have existed just like Balaam who had a relationship with God but whose paths never crossed Israel and therefore remain unknown to us today?

So, this is my point: of all the prophets and of all those who God acknowledged as His worshippers, there are some we see who the Israelites may have condemned, according to their ways, as non-children of God, as "Gentiles", as "uncircumcised". Yet, we can see that there may have been many, many others who also walked and talked and honoured the Almighty, that I am sure existed outside of the records of the children of Abraham. While Israel was in Egypt, While Abraham was walking with God, there were a lot of other people also walking with God who aren't recorded – at least not in the Books we have chosen to read and believe.

A friend once said, **"Don't read everything you believe".**

We can even go further ahead to the time after Jesus had come and gone where we meet a certain man called [8]Cornelius, described as a man who "feared God with his household and prayed continually to God." Obviously God heard and communed with him, but was he a Jew? Certainly not.

You must understand that each of these people is mentioned only as a side story to Abraham (or his descendants the Jews) and yet, it is indeed possible that they each have a more complete but unknown story about them. If any of these people we know and honour as prophets or children of God had a book written about them, would it be of any less effect than the Holy Books we have? Rather, a more appropriate question is, would you accept it as a book of instruction?

My point to you is simple, the things within the Holy Book are sacred but it doesn't mean that the things outside them aren't. Not such an easy pill to swallow is it? But think about it for a second, let it sink beyond the age long prejudice you hold.

---

[8] Acts 10

Apply reason. It isn't so unreasonable is it? In fact, it probably makes more sense than you would want it to.

This isn't about what is or isn't written outside the Holy Books you have. It's about understanding why what you have in the Holy Books is there in the first place. It's about realising that the Holy Books have many stories about things we should know and sometimes, in-between the lines, they have stories that aren't written that we should infer.

I do not ask that you go and deliberately seek out strange knowledge of what is outside the Holy Books, I only ask that a portion of your mind be used to process information in such a way that you do not exclude something because it's new or uncomfortable.

Humans have excelled in knowledge and we now know so much about so much. But we also know that on very many physical fronts, our knowledge is far less than complete. I have a favourite illustration that I use to show that despite the abundance of our knowledge of everything, there are some seemingly simple things we still can't understand. The illustration is the pendulum on a pendulum or double pendulum concept in

Mathematics. If you have a pendulum with known mass and known length of string, you can predict with exactness the pendulum's position at any point in time. However, once you attach another pendulum to the pendulum, the motion becomes "chaotic".

POSSIBILITY OF A NEW IDEA

If you believe you know all that there is to, then any new information you get would immediately be discarded. If you however, understand that your knowledge is incomplete, then new information will be accepted and processed. With God, there are people who think their knowledge of Him and His ways is complete and therefore would not accept any real possibility of a knowledge of Him that differs from what they know. They find it impossible to come to terms with or process new information regarding Him.

You know, this is the same issue the Jews had in the time of Jesus. He came with something new that wasn't quite to the letter of what they had in the scripture and they therefore, rejected his preaching and Him altogether. They couldn't reason beyond their beliefs and the dogma they held. There was no room for outsiders, no room for new revelation, and no room for anything contrary to what they knew. There was no way they would accept anything outside of the scripture that the Almighty had handed down to them. And indeed He had. They believed they knew all they had to know and they even knew exactly how whatever new thing God would do, would be done and they therefore rejected the idea, possibility and fact that this new thing was very different from what they expected.

Modern day Christians are, sadly, no different. Just like the Jews, they find it hard to accept anything that doesn't come in the form and manner they expect. The Jews held on to their God given beliefs and doctrines despite the fact that Jesus set a higher standard and taught a much better and more fulfilling doctrine. To their detriment, they stubbornly refused to let go of what they had, what they knew, what they had been taught from birth - they closed their minds to change! They believed they knew all that ought to be known and therefore discarded, without reason any new possibilities.

The Jews simply could not accept that the God they knew and served would take their "inheritance", their "birthright" and open it up to outsiders like you and me! (Even Apostles like Peter struggled with this and God had to personally intervene to put him straight in the case of Cornelius.)

Fast forward 2000 years - we have some other groups of people who are holding on to doctrine, who are refusing to let go of what they know, who are holding on to what they have been taught for generations. We have people who are closing their minds to change and refuse to believe that God can open up his Kingdom to those they term "outsiders".

Many religions hold a false belief that their way is the ONLY way and anyone not following their closed idea of who or what God is, is doomed. However, the group I will like to focus on goes by the name "Christian"!!! This is despite the fact that very many in this group are simply churchgoers and have no idea what it truly means to be a Christian.

I weep as I see history repeat exactly the same mistakes of old. God is making some major changes to His relationship with mankind and those that should propagate and promote the good news are resisting it and destroying it with closed ears, eyes, hearts and minds.

I have met very many people who hold on to what they have as if there is absolutely no other. By all means, hold fast to that which you have and have received, but do not assume that what another man holds, simply because it is different from yours, is therefore wrong. Seek understanding, look for the merits in their stories, their experiences, and their worship and then see if the Almighty may also accord honour to what they do. In your heart, seek to know what the Almighty ultimately wants and that is the standard with which you may measure what any other person teaches or preaches or practices.

An important question I ask is this: "Can God make another way?"

I recall a group of Christians I met and asked this question of and their response was quite predictable. They referred me to the Holy Book where Jesus said, [9]"I am the way, the truth and the life". I pointed out to them that even though they were 100% correct, there was a possibility they only covered a part of the whole picture.

One key perspective that can make a whole lot of difference is in the definition of 'The Way". Does it mean a doorway through which you must pass?

---

[9] John 14:6

Or could it be a literal "follow my way, meaning my lifestyle, my teachings – the way of life I have left as an example". If you confine the meaning to a doorway, you will, by man's interpretation, immediately eliminate a lot of tongues and tribes and nations from ever accessing the Father. But if you expand it to be followers of His way of life, then, so many others would have access and the brotherhood and the Father's children would, again by man's definition, expand.

Something else that's important to notice is that Jesus mentioned 3 attributes, but many Christians insist on holding on to just one – The Way. Jesus also said I am "The Truth". It is certain that God seeks "true" worshippers and also "He is Spirit and those that worship Him must do so in spirit and in Truth". Could that statement – "I am the Truth"- mean a lot more than the surface translation we give? Besides, if you think about the statement from a position of logic, then let's look at it this way: Jesus first **defines** the subject and then equates it to other virtues:

Jesus = Way = Truth = Life and we know from logic that:

If A = B = C = D, then B =D, right?

So, the statement, "no one comes to the Father but by me", could have much deeper meaning than we have ordinarily understood.

I showed them all I just told you, how the Pharisees had their way that was 100% correct (at the time) and yet, instead of opening their minds to the real work and **intent** of the Almighty, closed it with doctrine and dogma. They closed it so much that when The Almighty revealed a new and even better way to them through Jesus, doctrine and dogma didn't allow them to see the truth. Even a simple thought on the "new way" being proposed they didn't spare, for if they did, it would have been apparent that this "new way" was indeed better, more peaceable and more encompassing. It was certainly more in line with the nature of the God they knew and already served. I showed this group of Christians that what the Jews had was indeed handed down to them from The Father and they held on to it and didn't budge. But they failed to see that while for thousands of years, holding on to it was the right thing to do, there came a time, when letting go became the right thing to do. They missed it.

I told these Christians that many of them, and I dare say most, are no different from the

Pharisees of old. Holding on to what they have that is absolutely correct, but not understanding the intent of why they have what they have, not understanding its purpose, not being able to discern that if the purpose and intent aren't met, the Almighty can and will open another door to make His Perfect Will be done.

I then asked them this: "if The Almighty made another way, a better way, a way that would more closely meet what we know His intent for mankind is, would they let go of what they already have? Or would they, like the Pharisees hold on to doctrine and dogma and habit?"

They were smart enough to reflect on it and leave instead of giving an answer. And I was satisfied that they were thoughtful and considering what I said.

I met one of them again shortly after and he asked me a question. He asked me what I meant by The Almighty making a better way. He had not been able to understand why the Almighty may change what he believed He had already perfected.

I could quite easily see his confusion. I had to make him quickly understand that I was not categorically saying that The Creator of all things had certainly created "another way" – it's not as if it isn't within His power to do so if he pleases. I then pointed out to him that his error in looking for the literal translation of my words is the same error the children of Israel made with the doctrines of Jesus and is the same error many Christians make today. I told the young man, I was showing him that he could not restrict the Eternal Father to his limited understanding of a Limitless God. I showed him that he had to understand purpose and then translate doctrine to fit in, and not the other way round. If the doctrine you have doesn't fit the purpose of God, then you trash the doctrine. But what we do is, we look at the doctrine and believe it leads to the purpose – this is wrong.

This will be a bold and extremely categorical statement, but if I don't make it, all I have taught and will teach, all I have known and been shown will be in vain: ***God's purpose TODAY, in this time and His motive for ALL men is simple: to draw ALL men to Himself; to reconcile Himself to ALL. Whatever doctrine you have held on to that makes this purpose impossible, is therefore to be debunked.***

Now, don't get me wrong, it doesn't mean that God has changed; it doesn't mean that light and darkness can co-exist; it doesn't mean that our filth as man will be tolerated: it just means that He will make it easy for us to come to Him.

Think about this, which way to the Almighty was easier? The way of the LAW in the Old Testament or the way of GRACE in the New?

Then imagine just for illustration, that the Old Testament didn't exist and what we know today as the New Testament, were the Old Testament. In which case, the way of GRACE being the way we know becomes the old way. Imagine then that God makes a new way that's easier than the way of GRACE. You know what would happen? (Please give it a thought before you jump to the conclusion that it isn't possible for anything to be easier than Grace). Christians would behave just like the Jews. The top leadership of the churches would resist it. They would huff and puff and tell us how God Himself spoke to them and told them what to do – like the Pharisees huffed and puffed and told of how God gave the laws to their fathers in the divine handwriting of God Himself. The leaders of today's churches would find loopholes, by throwing cunning questions and trials to see how this new way stands up to what they already have – like the Pharisees kept on testing Jesus to see how and when He would contradict some of their Laws. When the leaders cannot find any real fault, other than the fact that the way is new and not a way they are used to, they would kill it – like the Pharisees killed the bearer of the new way that was different from the way of the LAW.

But truth be told, without understanding the purpose of the Father, we are all at risk of this error and are possibly already making it in different spheres of our lives. We must all - all nations, all tribes, all tongues, all RELIGIONS - be sensitive to this and look for ways we can converge and not ways to divide. We must be sensitive to The Almighty's ultimate divine plan of reconciling mankind to Himself by any means He sees necessary.

MATCHSTICK, ROPE, VESSEL, POWDER

It had been a couple of weeks since I had seen Pa Abraham. I had been having an unbelievably busy schedule and I wasn't sure whether in meeting with him, I was enjoying exposing my ignorance on topics I felt I was a master. One thing I found rather bewildering though (and I'm still not sure if it's my over-reaching imagination), every time I left Pa Abraham, the rest of my day would go amazingly well. His words always had a way of springing a well within me; I always wanted to know more and in a funny way, I wanted to be like him.

There was no point depriving myself of good company and a feel good after-effect, so I called him to book another meeting. He mentioned that he was spending the evening on his boat and much to my delight; he said he would enjoy my company. Now that sounded more like it: cruising gently on the clear waters, watching the sun descend in golden glory, sipping on fine wine whilst being thoroughly drenched in a world of uncanny wisdom. Nothing sounded better.

I was at the jetty half an hour early, not to prove a point this time, but I wanted to watch him arrive and step out of the car. I wanted to observe him without his knowledge - I still had this nagging and slightly uncomfortable feeling at the back of my head that I couldn't accurately place. So, I sat in the car and waited…..and waited…and waited. Then there was a knock on the window – "sir, you are requested to come unto the boat now." For crying out loud, how did that happen? He certainly didn't come past me, his car wasn't there. Perhaps, just perhaps he lived on the boat. But how did they know it was me in the car?

As usual his broad and enchanting smile drew me all the way from the pier onto the simple but grand 42ft Sunseeker yacht. It had a small mahogany top table set for two with grilled lobster with mustard cheese sauce and fine French white wine laid with beautifully carved crystal glasses. Simplicity in the most elegant form.

I noticed he had some very old looking thick leather bound books in a small glass shelf. As I reached for one, he interrupted and said, "that's where I keep the Holy Books."

"I've been meaning to ask sir, you often refer to books - Plural? Surely you must align with only one religion."

"Yes books! Surely young man, whichever inclination you choose to tilt towards, you do not seriously believe there's only one holy book?"

I recalled he made a similar comment at breakfast weeks back, and I had let it slide as a slip; but clearly there was more to it than I had thought. However, I didn't feel like answering and he didn't press. We ate in silence as if we wanted to take in as much of the beauty of the scenery - the calming sound of the water and the cool, clean salt laden air.

No matter how your day ended, some things will certainly lift your spirit like watching the sun descend slowly into the horizon with its golden rays stretching across the waters, gazing at winged creatures having a last sip from the ocean then gracefully gliding to their nests and sipping the finest French wine while listening to the powerful buzz of heavy twin powered 660hp engines.

Finally he asked about my day. It had been a weird day but in summary, I felt like I had achieved a great deal more than I was recognised for and I had expected a lot more than I got.

He smiled and said that he knew a story that he felt I needed to hear. It was the story of a farmer, a matchstick, an empty vessel and gunpowder. Awkward combination, but that's Pa Abraham for you.

"A farmer had toiled his whole life with very little to show for it, he barely got by daily and he constantly prayed and asked for blessings from The Creator. One day he decided, after experiencing a terrible drought that took all that he had, that there was nothing more to live for. He decided that he would take all he had left in his cart, go up a nearby mountain and arrange a personal, unscheduled appointment with his Creator.

"Close to the top of the mountain, he noticed a rather large rock and behind the rock was a clear lake fed by a nearby spring. He paused for a minute and then leaned over to drink what he believed was his last. Suddenly he realised that if he moved the rock, the stream would flow downhill and nourish his drought laden land. He thought about moving the boulder for a long while. He then untied the rope from the cart and stuffed it into some gunpowder in a vessel he had in his belongings. He buried the vessel holding the gunpowder deep into a crevice in the rock, brought out a matchstick and then lit the rope. The blast dislodged the rock.

"His farm was saved. His life was saved. With a constant supply of fresh water, his farm became the best producing in the land and within a few years, he was the wealthiest farmer in that part of the country."

"Nice story", I said with a little bit of sarcasm, "kinda predictable." I could have sworn I saw I tinge of hurt in his eyes and I suspect I was a little too gleeful that I had one up on him. Pa Abraham smiled and said, "yes, it would seem too predictable because you are focusing on the farmer. The story isn't about him."

"How do you sit me here for half an hour, tell me a story about a depressed farmer that suddenly struck it big and then say the story isn't about him? Oh, let me guess, it's about the how the lobster drank too much wine and ended up on our plates, right?"

"Each human has an element of the matchstick, the rope, the vessel and the gunpowder in them. The story, my son, is about you."

I'm not sure which was more annoying; that this old man felt he knew enough of me to concoct a whole tale, or that the silly tale didn't even have any glamour. But hey, we had a beautiful sunset, great wine, fine lobster – I'm sure I could indulge him for a few more hours to see where the story went.

THE MATCHSTICK

"My son, the matchstick represents the spark I see when I look in your eyes; a spark which holds the inherent fear that once you light the match, it would be used up and gone. You also worry that a mere spark isn't enough to make the type of impact and difference you want and so, you prefer to keep the match hidden, sheltered and unused believing that you're waiting for the perfect moment when it is needed. You fear its glow and lifespan will be short lived, it will fade and you will be lost. So, your keenly treasured and guarded asset and being, becomes the one thing you never use.

"The story tells you that a single matchstick can initiate a series of reactions that can cause an effect far beyond the power that lies within it. Let me use the example of light. A matchstick can indeed light the whole world, given the right timing, conditions and the important precondition that it must be lit in the first place.

"You wonder about the purpose of your life and the answer to that is akin to a seed existing in the fruit and the fruit in the seed. The answer lies in the question and the question in the answer. Light your match, ignite a fire and see what contagion you let loose upon the world.

"A matchstick cannot be of any meaningful use if it's never lit. It must be willing to burn itself out and must be able to transfer its energy and light to others that can either carry it or use it.

"It is important to realise that a matchstick cannot fulfill its purpose if its priority is self-preservation.

"Some of us are designed to sacrifice ourselves for the greater good of a cause, a people, society or venture. Some of us must train ourselves to share our light, give our power and transfer our strength to those that can carry it on further, longer and more effectively than we ever can, long after we are gone. It is our responsibility to train ourselves to seek such people out. And so my son, I'm hoping that you are beginning to understand our meeting and our relationship.

"A matchstick sitting in utter and complete darkness may wonder of what use his transient glow would be and would wonder what difference his spark could make. But once he is willing to give himself, he will then see that the room is full of candles waiting and hoping he would give them his light to carry on. Each is praying that he would end his selfish self-abasement and produce a spark that would be carried by them throughout time. The matchstick signifies the beginning of the end for darkness. The matchstick is indeed powerful."

"It truly is amazing how you do that sir!" This time around I couldn't hold the thought in. "It's as if you know my deepest thoughts and you strike right at them. I have always felt I had a lot to share but I have always been worried that I'd be giving up myself wrongly and I would be wasted."

"My son, wait! Hear the whole lesson."

THE ROPE

"It would have made sense to use examples of candles and lamps to illustrate the lessons but I have chosen the rope, vessel and gunpowder because of what I see in you - the unique and powerful qualities that have both driven and hindered you."

My own tailor-made-life-fulfilling story, I thought. Yay! Ok, I know I'm being a brat.

"In this story, the rope is a carrier. I can imagine your confusion with seeing the rope as a carrier when we also have a vessel in the equation. Just listen a while longer and you will understand. I have chosen the rope to show you that though you have many great and useful talents, you must know which one would make the most impact on humanity. A rope can be used to bind, to hold down, to drag and to oppress. In a society such as yours, these may be desirable qualities to maintain law and order and sometimes even provide direction, but a rope also has a unique ability to be a carrier. It can be used to transfer power from a matchstick to gunpowder. It can be the bridge that connects the seemingly insignificant spark to the latent powerhouse.

"The rope had been useful all its life to the farmer for holding the cart together. Whilst this was a noble and, at the time, a relevant task, the rope must be able to become adaptable to changing situations and calls for higher responsibility even when it means its existence may cease."

THE GUNPOWDER

"Gunpowder certainly has no visually attractive quality that would make any normal person desire to keep it. If anything at all, it looks a lot like sand or dirt. Sitting on a shelf without a tag along with other items such as stones or rocks or even rubbish, gunpowder would almost certainly be passed over. Its power, quality and usefulness aren't found in its ability to sit on a shelf or in being out in the open. Its quality and power are most exhibited when it is constrained and cramped in a tight space (or vessel) and loaded with a lot of pressure.

"The gunpowder holds unbelievable potential and awesome power which can be used for one or two purposes – creation or destruction – it all depends on whose hands the trigger is placed in. In itself, it would seem like a completely harmless substance and you can jolly well play with it and toss it around with little risk. However, the moment you bring it in contact with a spark, you'd find that that harmless substance can be dangerously powerful. The power you can realise would be even more, if you compact it (similar to restraining it, putting it under pressure and confining it to a rather uncomfortable situation) and then add the spark.

"The real secret of gunpowder is knowing how and when to use it."

THE VESSEL

"The vessel, my son, is the quality you have that you must watch carefully. Your self-confidence is a beauty to witness when you soar and show it with the unalloyed integrity you possess. But my son, there is a thin line from where you stand to where you may fall. Your subtle vanity, arrogance and conceit are exposed in the lessons about the vessel. The beautifully crafted vessel attaches a great deal of self-importance to itself and believes that it is too good or too smart for certain roles while considering itself too important for tasks, missions or operations that it feels do not glorify it directly. It looks for acknowledgement and praise and something even close to worship.

"The vessel is the last piece of the puzzle that makes the whole thing come together. In this story, it has a seemingly small and insignificant task that brings it no obvious glory: to hold the dirty gunpowder compact and intact. But it is the one that keeps the power broker, if you want to call it that, in check - holding the power but not being the power. This is similar to playing second fiddle to the one it would normally look down on, the dirty looking and ignored one, the one it would normally feel isn't comparable in elegance and intelligence and craftsmanship.

"I picture you willingly giving up tasks you view as menial and lose sight of the potential such tasks have in inspiring a cause beyond a reach you could ever attain.

"Now, back to the context of the story. The vessel felt it was too good to be used for anything other than serving kings. It was disgusted that all this time it was used to carry such a dirty thing as gunpowder and dreamed of when its lost glory would be restored – when it would be in a special place used by special people to bring fine wine and joy and laughter to all. Now, the gunpowder was understandably upset and felt rather insulted because it knew it had so much power within it and yet being confined to such a tight space was beneath its potential. It felt that if set free and spread around it would more than conquer the world. The rope was coiled in a corner and reminisced on all the stories it had heard of how its type had been used to conquer great cities, how its kind had been used to hold down and conquer giants. It was dejected and moaned that it had never been used for any great feat except to drag around an old cart. The matchstick on the other hand, was full of energy and hope and ambition. It wanted to make a difference and believed that it would, one day, be part of a move to bring light to all and was saving itself for that. It had just a little spark and didn't want to waste it. It had to make sure it was used at the right time and in the right way.

"They all had gigantic dreams, they all sensed there was a bigger plan, a more respectable way to utilise their skills and a more powerful way to harness their potential: but in the meantime, staying alone, they all achieved nothing, they just waited and dreamed."

THE COMMON THEME

"All the elements must be self-sacrificial to bring the change they want to see.

"It is painfully hilarious sitting back and watching the four instruments argue, bicker and fight with each other over who is greater, who is more important and the worst of all arguments, who the farmer prefers and what the farmer will do and what he thinks about and what his nature is.

"Put yourself in the position of the farmer who brought all of them together for a specific purpose based on their individual strengths and qualities. Imagine how he would feel watching them destroy each other because they have different understandings of who he is or what his intent is. Imagine his pain as they maim themselves, cut short their destinies, refuse to work with each other and then individually come to him and "lobby" him to ignore everyone else and use only one.

"The farmer knows that he needs each of them exactly as they are and the farmer knows anyone of them changing to become another would interrupt his plan. Because he sees that if they refuse to work together his ultimate desire would not be met, in his mercy, wisdom and so that his purpose is fulfilled, he reasons with them, assuages them, even gives them what they want – but only to the end that his purpose is fulfilled.

"We humans can barely fathom the complexities, possibilities and potential of the human brain nor the beauty and splendor of nature. We are still studying with a hope of understanding, natural phenomena like tornadoes, fire whirls, the morning glory and Catatumbo Lightning. Even some simple medical conditions, like the Hiccup, remained mysteries till recently and some still amaze and befuddle medical science.

"The Hubble telescope can see out to over 10 billion light years (for perspective, that's 58,656,9 60,000,000,000,000,000,000 miles, and the moon is 250,000 miles from the earth). We have all sorts of technology and gadgets and yet, the Malaysian MH370 "vanished" from radar and with all our fantastic technology, we still couldn't locate nor even calculate where it would have crashed. Despite the explosion of knowledge since the 17th century, our knowledge about our universe, the human body and even the very earth we inhabit is still very limited. The more we explore, the more we find and it seems like there's no end in sight to the magnificence of everything the Almighty created.

"I believe that our knowledge of Him is extremely limited and I'd postulate that the ratio of the earth to the universe would be roughly the same ratio as all our combined knowledge of Him is compared to what He really is.

"With all these, it's truly amazing when we hear and witness people who suppose they "know" and "understand" the Creator whilst their knowledge of the created is so limited. Though we can see the human body, dissect it and study, though we have the earth and weather and atmosphere with us and we have scientists devoting their entire lives to studying all the naturally occurring phenomena, yet, we still haven't scratched the surface of knowledge. I never cease to wonder therefore, when I listen to various religious scholars who attempt to teach, in definite and conclusive language, about the Almighty they have never seen, nor studied nor even have a full picture of. They speak of Him as if they created Him and not the other way round. They tell us of His likes, dislikes, habits and conditions in terms that they wouldn't even be able to use to describe themselves.

The Almighty Father, creator of the universe, creator of our bodies & brains and commander of nature certainly doesn't need us to protect nor fight for Him. He most certainly doesn't need man to portray Him as anything other than what He has chosen to reveal Himself as. Regarding His nature and His Being, we are on a very strict "need to know" basis and we assume, foolishly, and to our own destruction, that the little we know is all there is to know.

"One of the Holy Books states, "In the beginning God said, Let US create man…" I have pondered over the years as to the composition of "US" in that statement and no, all my intellect cannot come to an answer that remotely seems to make sense. I know as a human, "US" must mean more than one personality for we are taught that "US" is plural. But how many exactly does that represent? The Christian folk will largely say 3 and even if we agree that we can identify 3 personalities that could make up the "US", it doesn't mean that there are only 3 – it simply means we are aware of and can contemplate only 3. There could be 50, there could be 2. (I personally think it's not less than 8)

"The point is we cannot possibly know more about the unseen and unobservable Creator of the Universe than we do about the universe itself. So when I see people bicker and argue over what God's intentions are regarding various religions, I cannot but laugh.

"The one thing I know about God, our Creator, is that He wants to have a relationship with us and sin, which He hates, precludes that. And so, anything that brings mankind closer to Him, anything that removes sin and anyone that abhors sin will certainly get His attention and blessing.

"Why then do we, mere mortals, create disputes over how and who and what is acceptable to Him and in what manner we should do this or that?

"He created us all different for a specific purpose; we have our various beliefs that all should work congruently; and yet we spend our time despising those that are different and we go around attempting to make us all the same.

"Of what use would the gunpowder be if the rope convinced it to become a rope? Or of what value would the vessel be if he saw the matchstick and decided to change? The farmer needs the rope to be the rope as he does the matchstick to be a matchstick. The farmer expects that they would all understand and trust that He has chosen them that way because His use of them is tied to their nature. If the matchstick refuses to work with the rope and prefers to work with the vessel instead, of what use would that be to the farmer?

"We must be wise, we must understand and we must see that the infinite wisdom of the Father cannot be comprehended by the human mind. We must find ways and reasons for unity and convergence of thought and not destroy each other because we are different.

"What then is the purpose of the Creator? What is your mission within His purpose?"

A.S.K.

[10]*"Ye ask and do not receive because you ask amiss ...."*

Pa Abraham continued, "There aren't many people who will dispute that life is a journey that starts when you are born but doesn't end when you die.

"I like to repeat a saying I heard many years ago that **"Life is merely a dream and you wake up at death".** Living our lives with this in mind would make us a lot more fulfilled.

"I spent many years studying and seeking out what the purpose of life is. I travelled to many places, I met so many people, encountered deep life changing experiences and yet, life's purpose eluded me. Till one day, sitting stranded on one of my many journeys I began to play back my entire

---

[10] James 4:3(NKJV)

life story: all those who had helped me, all those I had helped, the things I had learnt, the people I had hurt and how I so wanted to make things right with them, those who had hurt me and how I felt better knowing I had forgiven them. I recalled the many things I did that made me ashamed and the many more I didn't do that I really should have done.

"Suddenly, a rather simple pattern struck me. In my entire life, I had regrets for only the things that left either no impact or a negative impact on others and I had pride in the things that left a positive memory or had a positive impact or I knew would have a lasting benefit to others.

"That was it.

"The purpose of life is really not as complicated as I had thought but it took the seeking to realise that.

"The purpose of life is to live a life of purpose. The real question though is, to what end?

"Imagine you met a very rich man of whom the fame of his wealth has been told to all nations, a rich man who had the resources to do anything he pleased and buy whatever houses and cars and businesses he so desired. Imagine you met such a man and he took a deep liking to you and over time, you developed a great trusting friendship with him. Meanwhile you, on the other hand, have been oppressed over the years working so very hard with little to show for it; feeling like you have failed yourself and your family and even considered taking your life to end the struggle, disappointments and misery. Imagine then, one day while you are toiling in the heat of the day, breaking your back trying to earn your daily bread, wondering when the suffering and torment and penury would end, you receive a very elaborate letter, written as a scroll with trimmings of gold and arriving in a mahogany box clearly carved by the best hands in the world and the letter reads thus:

> *"My dear friend, I have oft thought about you since our meeting and I long for your company to share time with you and discuss the things I know nothing about but you so deeply understand. You have struck me as an upright man who hasn't been fortunate enough to have seen the good things of*

life despite your hard labours, prudence and determination. Today, as I sat in my room, I decided within myself to use all I have to reward just men like you. Men who, despite the hardship the world has bestowed on them have continued to work and fend for their family in every way possible without complaining and without denting their conscience. Today my friend, I have prepared a city with many houses and gardens and workers and every need you and your family would ever imagine has been stored up for you. You deserve it my friend and I happily bestow it on you. There is only one condition you must meet; make a simple request of me that I shall grant."

"Imagine that you received such an awesome letter which pretty much leaves you with a blank cheque from an account with limitless funds. Ask yourself in sincerity and clearness of mind, what would that one request be?

"Would you be so predictably human as to make a mundane request based on a fleeting immediate need, or rather, desire? Would you see this as an opportunity to satisfy a long held lust whose consequence is in any case, nothing but further emotional agony? Would you request a pay rise for the many hours you toil? Or perhaps you would prefer to obtain a promotion at work? Perchance a bigger farm upon which to toil some more? Would you ask for a bigger bed to lay your head? Maybe even, you would wish ill or death to the men who had so despitefully used you over the years? Maybe you'd ask for more children, smarter children or a larger house? Or more wives? A car, private jet, or just much more in riches? What would that request be?

"Whatever you ask for at this point will say everything about what you believe and what you prioritise.

"Let's allow this scenario to properly sink into our consciousness because it isn't in any way fictional. ***There's no better way to know the depth (or shallowness) of a man's heart's desires than to ask to grant him his wishes.*** There's an infinite amount of wisdom to be garnered from studying and especially, following the way of life of Jesus Christ.

"He constantly told His disciples (and all who acknowledge Him as the "WAY") that He was going away to prepare a place for them and He spent time describing this place and expecting that they (all His followers) would all be overjoyed at the prospects and possibilities of living in paradise. He also spoke about how man would always set his heart to where his treasure lay and He tried to tell us to become spiritual beings and therefore have spiritual treasures because that then would be where we would set our hearts.

"I look around today and putting these teachings together, I can very easily deduce that there aren't many people who believe that there is a paradise. Yes, if you asked they would all answer that they believe there is paradise but from their behaviour and priorities, it's easy to tell they believe otherwise. Like the famous late Afrobeat musician Fela said, "we all want to go to heaven but no one wants to die." I cannot imagine how men can live the lives they do if they truly believed that life and possessions on earth happen to be transient. It is **impossible** to set yourself a goal for sometime in the future and insist on dwelling in the present and yet hope to attain the goal. IMPOSSIBLE. But that's what I see mankind do.

"Ok, that may be harsh and many will kick against it so perhaps I should rephrase and say, "There are not many who believe that the treasures laid up in paradise are any better than those on earth." If truly a man's heart and his desires are tied to where his treasures are, from the way I see even pastors, laying up treasures in banks and property here on earth, I do not think they have any intention of making it to paradise. Emphasis is in "LAYING UP" – "accumulating", "protecting" their "treasures" even going as far as hiring armed body guards. They obviously truly and vehemently love life on earth and want to hold on as long as possible. I speak not against the owning of assets, but I stand firmly against the accumulation to extravagant amounts **at the expense of** living as a spiritual being. No, it is not a condition that you be poor to make it to heaven, but of a truth, the more assets you acquire beyond your needs, the more likely you will set your treasures here on earth and not in heaven and therefore the harder it will be to get in there. Remember the camel and the eye of the needle?

"Personally, I would expect that anyone with a one-way ticket to a better place than where he was would very quickly use it and not spend time trying to accumulate assets that would have no impact on your impending journey.

"Let's ignore other people and go back to the teachings of Jesus for a minute.

"Follow the chain of thought here – First we are sure that God has prepared a better place with treasures for all His servants and we have been taught that your heart will always lie where your treasure is, or at least where you believe it is.

"Jesus taught another concept that is extremely powerful when tied to these two that have already been mentioned i.e. the concept of making requests.

He said, "[11]**A**sk, and it will be given to you; **S**eek, and you will find; **K**nock, and it will be opened to you." I will agree that it is probably a coincidence that the first letters of ask, seek and knock actually spell out "ASK", but allow me ride on that for a minute because it will also give insight to the fact that the combination of all three would give you a complete request.

"I had always thought that those were three different ways to make requests from the Almighty and indeed they can be. But, if you remember the 2 principles we just spoke about and you infuse

---

[11] Matthew7:7 (NKJV)

this into them, it has a whole new meaning. In this context, asking, seeking and knocking aren't really 3 distinct ways of making requests, they are in fact the directions and instructions for making the perfect singular request. Within themselves, they show you the exact request to make. They are the solution the comment below:

"[12]Ye ask and do not receive because you ask amiss….."

"Let's now put all three precepts together: Your treasure is in paradise, your heart is with your treasure and you need to make a request of the Almighty, what would that request be? I hope it now sounds pretty straightforward.

"If I called you and told you I had made complete provision for your entire life, that everything you ever wanted was already provided and available and all you had to do was pick up the keys; I believe the very next thing you would do would be to **ASK** one specific question: you would ask for my location, or my address or how to get to me in order to get the keys. If you asked that, I would give you an address, but in the context we are discussing, directions would make a lot more sense. I would give you directions on how to get to me. After such

---

[12] James4:3 (NKJV)

a discussion, it would then be rather awkward to make any request whose purpose or outcome would be focused on keeping you comfortable in your present location or any request that pertains to cementing your relationship with anything in your present location – unless of course, that's where your treasure is and therefore, your heart.

"So, first you would ASK for my location and how to get to me, then having obtained directions, you would, reasonably, proceed on a journey to find the address – that is, you would then **SEEK** me out. The directions and journey aren't on a smooth paved road. There's some trouble on the way because there are people (or forces) that will not sleep trying to make sure you do not find your way to me – but I have already assured you that all you need for the journey is provided and you should not worry or fret about the obstacles you encounter on the journey. I also tell you that, though you do not see me, it is a pathway I have previously treaded and I will be guiding you all the way. I would also request that as you seek me, you must be diligent and patient and you must not give up. The precept about your heart being where your treasures are would ensure that you do not faint on the journey.

"When you finally reach the destination the directions led you to, and you see the house number on the door, it really won't make sense to sit outside and hope someone opens the door. You would **KNOCK** at which point, your host, your Heavenly Father, would be only too glad to open up the door.

"The important point to note in all of this is that the Father expects the entire purpose of your request of Him to be for the purpose of getting to Him; this is what I believe He means when He says, "asking according to His will." Everything else is a distraction not just for you, but also for Him. His end point, His purpose, His "WAY" is unidirectional and with singularity of purpose –finding your way back to Him.

"Whoever you are, wherever you are, whatever you think, whatever you do or have done, whatever your tribe or religion or disposition, as long as you are human, God our Creator has only one purpose for your life – to get back to Him - and you have only one issue preventing that purpose - sin. Everything you encounter in life is either from Him to help you achieve that purpose or from the enemy to prevent you from achieving the purpose. Truth be told, it's really not hard discerning which is which. Simply ask yourself: will it help you get to Him or will it make you want to stay where you are? Does the end result of your current state of being result in helping you achieve God's singular purpose or not?"

A NEW BIRTH (BORN AGAIN)

I have had many conversations and debates about the most obscure topics and I usually come out on top. This is not because I'm any better than the next person, but I happen to know a little about a lot of things; and of course, I only engage people who know a whole lot about very little. Then I keep the subject away from what they already know. I call this the "illusion of intelligence" – taking on people in the areas they are weakest and because they are generally very learned, they will therefore assume you are, at least, as learned as them. That illusion, played often enough eventually becomes reality. You will then understand how intriguing it is to have a discussion on a topic I feel I am conversant with and yet, I am made to look quite ignorant.

So, Pa Abraham asked me on some fine evening why I was not born again. But who in this day and age goes to church and is not a born again Christian? We all believe in Jesus Christ; that he shed his blood, died and rose again. We are all born again Christians, are we not?

But then, Pa Abraham said, "Young man, **you cannot add to a full cup.** To learn, you must first come to a place where you believe you have something to receive. If you know it all, there's nothing new to know and if what you know is folly, you will die in your folly and what's worse, you will live in that same folly. It's almost certainly better for you to actually die in that folly and certainly better for the rest of humanity. Empty your cup of half-baked knowledge and see what new and wonderful experience you can attain."

So, considering I have spent the last decade or two going to church an average of twice a week, I believed I knew the Bible fairly well and prayed often. I was certainly not as bad as most of the other hypocrites, fraudsters and evil people I see all around. In fact, I'd go as far as saying I was a rather good person. So it was somewhat hard on my ego asking the question, but I did, of course tweaking it not to completely show my newly accepted ignorance. "Pa, what is your understanding of the concept of being born again?"

That priceless smile lit up his face again.

"May I ask you a question as well? What is your understanding?"

I think he saw the confounded look on my face and he moved swiftly to take me away from that uncomfortable place of ignorance. I bet he's done this many times based on the swiftness with which he moved on. I could swear he could see my heart dislodge from my rib cage and head towards my rectum.

He rephrased to, "Who was the message of being born again directed at?"

Phew. "Nicodemus the Jew...errr...Pharisee; elder of the people, well educated in the scriptures."

Answering the much easier version of his question in such detail, I felt like the biggest success inhuman history.

"So", Pa Abraham goes, "Nicodemus was asked to be born all over again, by water and the spirit – notice though, not water and blood. Interestingly, the actual Greek word used in that conversation is **anagennaó** meaning to **beget into a new life.** This is one of the very few instances Jesus spoke literally and from the response of Nicodemus, it was obvious the request was rather absurd. But then, He wouldn't have asked Nicodemus to do the impossible, that just won't make sense, would it?

"Being born again doesn't require anything more than what Jesus said. Now, what he said may require process and have a deeper meaning, but He certainly doesn't make a request for you to change your religion; at least He didn't request that from anyone. That's something we ought to understand and meditate on deeply. But let's deal with that a little later.

"To make being born again easy to conceptualise, it would be important to first answer the question "what does it mean to be born"? For if you know and fully appreciate what being born means, then, it would be easy to know what being born (all over) again is. For the same rules and process will be followed, just from a spiritual and not physical context. Do you ask anyone for evidence that the person is born? That would be rather absurd – "hello sir, do you mind if I ask you to prove that you were truly born?" Yeah, you may wish to know when or where or by whom he was born, but you certainly won't ask if he were born at all. His mere existence is the evidence. When he enters a room or has a conversation, you would know immediately that a living person exists and has walked into your presence.

"Now also, when you are born, you spend almost all of your early to mid life learning and growing. You must learn all the various laws that are relevant to make your existence possible, productive as well as comfortable. First the laws of your environment, the laws of your body, the laws of the universe in which you exist and then the laws of the land where you live. You'd learn the importance of and relationships between food, sleep and exercise. You'd learn the correlation between diet and weight, diet and energy levels and if you're like me, you'd learn the correlation between diet and mood.

"You'd also learn the laws of gravity and of the seasons, you'd go to school and learn the laws in respect of cohabitation with the opposite sex; you'd learn the laws of your body - internal and external and of course, the laws of reward and consequence. Laws, laws, laws and rules, rules, rules – you'd keep learning to make sure that your human being exists in perfect harmony with your environment. In a nutshell, that's what happens when you are born. You don't stop learning, you don't stop growing and you don't stop adapting.

"As you mature and form your belief system, you would also learn that the fact that you do not believe in certain laws has no effect on the consequence of the law. If you don't believe in the Law of Gravity and you therefore step off the roof of a 10-storey building to prove your disbelief in the law, the ground rushing towards you will certainly convince you, even if it's too late, that you were wrong to disbelieve the law.

"It is vitally important to understand that when you are born again, the same process replicates within your spirit being. You are born of the Spirit of God and irrespective of your earthly age, you are a brand new spiritual being existing in a different realm under a different set of laws and all the laws, you must learn anew over time. Like when you are born, some laws you will learn from your (spiritual) environment, some others you will learn from (spiritually) older people who can teach and mentor you, but most importantly, you will learn the most from your parents (Heavenly Father) of whose Spirit you are now born.

"The laws of spiritual nature and nurture, the laws of handling the conflicts between the spiritual and the physical, the laws of communication and the laws of creative powers, the laws of the power in the words you speak. You never know all the laws, just like in the physical life. You stumble on some, some take time to understand and some take time to master. Some people are more conversant with the laws in Physics while others are more conversant with the laws of human behaviour. So it is spiritually; so don't be disturbed that others know a lot more than you in some spiritual field. We are not meant to all know the same things.

"As a 10 year old knows everything he has been taught and in his mind thinks he knows "everything" there is to know without realising he has only been shown a glimpse of the world; the same happens to Christians. They know what they have been exposed to and therefore think they know all there is to.

The Bible says (and this is the reason why), [13]"pride goeth before destruction and let him that thinketh he standeth take heed lest he fall."

"Being born again is a consciousness. It's understanding that ***you are no longer a human being with a spirit, but a spirit being in a human.*** It means that you now operate under a totally different set of

---

[13] Proverbs 16:18; 1 Corinthians 10:12

laws; laws you must seek out, learn, understand, practice, teach and submit to.

"When you realise you are a spirit being living as a human, you will know you still need to care for both laws: the spirit laws and the physical laws – but more for the spirit laws because spirit laws control the physical. Whereas, when you were a human being merely with a spirit, you only cared for the physical laws.

"When you are born again, no one will ask you if you are, just as no one asks you if you were born. Your mere [spiritual] existence would be evidence that you are. Everyone you interact with regularly will notice there's something about you that makes you different and they will want to ask, "what happened to you?" There will be a distinct and noticeable difference and it will exude from your personality. People will notice that your concern for physical laws has diminished while your concern for spiritual laws has increased.

"How about zombies?"That was my weak and desperate attempt at humor to mask my growing realization of my ignorance.

"Well, as there are zombies – dead humans with no spirit, there are also spiritual zombies – dead spirits that merely exist but truly are already dead. That is why when you are born again, that is, born of the Spirit, the Spirit will "quicken" you – make you alive, bring you out of the realm of being a spiritual zombie.

"Our natural inclination as a people in this part of the world is more akin to a gerontocracy and that ideology, or culture if you like, is unfortunately extended into the church. We fail to see that as spiritual beings, physical age is totally and absolutely irrelevant. We often confuse and/or correlate physical age with spiritual maturity and that has over the years, constantly put us in a terrible bind. We expect that the older you are, then the faster you learn the spiritual laws and therefore see younger ones as less experienced. Remember that Jesus, at just 12 years old, confounded the elderly scholars with His knowledge of the scripture.

"Frankly, it's just as ridiculous as saying a particular child will outgrow and out-mature another simply because his parents are 60 years old and the parents of the other are 40. As a man becomes born all over again, he becomes as a child spiritually and must learn and grow. Perhaps he will grow faster based on his spiritual diet, but certainly not based on his physical age. This is a key reason why the concept of humility is paramount in anyone who truly is a child of God. It is the understanding that you do not know a man's spiritual maturity till he speaks and acts, and you must be willing and humble to first listen and watch. You must be willing to accept that though he may look small and inexperienced and more "lowly" compared to you, he may very well be a "master" in the eyes of God and may be one of spiritual authority.

"So, back to being born again. I remember as a young man, I almost had my head taken off when I started speaking on this concept. I remember pointing out that Jesus asked Nicodemus to be born again…that's all. The entire request. Full stop. He didn't invite him to a denomination, He didn't ask him to change anything, and He didn't ask him to leave what he was. He simply asked him to become born of the Spirit. Interestingly, this would have meant that Nicodemus would have been a born again Jew. And if there were Gentiles hearing the message and accepting, they too would have been born again Gentiles. As mentioned earlier, being born spiritually (again) has quite some parallels with being born physically: Some are born black, some white, some mixed race, some tall, short and it goes on – key difference is that you are a born again spirit – not anything else.

"So many who the Heavenly Father would have so happily embraced as children, so many who would have willingly turned their lives and beings over to God their Creator, have walked away disappointed because they were given an illegitimate condition to approaching Him – a requirement to first change their "religion". That requirement even if not expressly stated by those preaching, is almost always implied.

"Mahatma Gandhi is one well-known classic example:

"When asked by a missionary why he quoted Christ so much but rejected being his "follower", he replied, *"Oh, I don't reject your Christ. I love your Christ. It is just that so many of you Christians are so unlike your Christ."*

"I can just imagine how I would feel if someone told me something as ridiculous as my requiring to first change my race or nationality or accent to be able to receive a certain gift."

What Pa Abraham was saying certainly made logical sense, but it just didn't make the kind of sense I was used to and it wasn't what I'd been conditioned to hear and understand. But no doubt, it made sense.

He continued, "if indeed you are born all over again into a different realm, you must follow the rules for growth, development and existence in that realm and, unless and until you are born into the realm, you really wouldn't know what the people in the realm are like.

"Being born again is about transferring your consciousness from the physical to the spiritual. As a matter of fact, everything about worship is clearly about transcending from here (earth) to there (God's presence). The more I read about the teachings in the Holy Books and particularly those of Jesus, the more I realise that we are all physical beings without any understanding of what it really means to worship the Father in Spirit. We attempt to deny our bodies of food and other physical pleasures to increase our spiritual experience but more than anything else, on a daily basis, we must have a permanent consciousness of God in our minds and hearts. The same way that a self-preservative-consciousness on an instinctive level compels us to cover our noses when we smell something really pungent (even though in reality, as long as we still breathe, that covering doesn't do much). It is the same level of instinct that we must attain spiritually. We must instinctively protect our spirit from "pungent" thoughts, behaviors and associations. It is only when we have a consciousness of the spirit and a deep consciousness of being children in the service of God that this becomes possible.

"Retaining the consciousness of God in your spirit means you will only look out and care for the things that matter to your Father – and I can assure you, the things that matter to Him, aren't the things that matter to us (as physical beings). The consciousness of God is the key to understanding Him and this gives us the ability to worship Him in Spirit, the only form of worship that He truly desires and enjoys."

TRUE WORSHIP

"Now", Pa Abraham said, "let's examine how to worship God.

"There's a curious phrase in one of the Holy Books, [14]"But the hour is coming, and now is, when the true worshipers will worship the Father in spirit and truth; for the Father is seeking such to worship Him." In other words, **IT IS TIME.**

"In grammar, they call that phrase Present Continuous I believe. From now on without end.

"The full story in the chapter from which that passage is derived describes a time when Jesus, contrary to the religious dictates at the time, had a conversation by a well with a woman from Samaria. To fully appreciate the depth of the conversation between Jesus and the Samaritan woman, it

---

[14] John 4:23 (NKJV)

is **EXTREMELY** important to understand the substance of the relationship, or rather, lack of, between the Jews and the Samaritans. It's not enough to know they hated each other so much so that they were not even allowed to speak with each other.

"According to history and genealogy, the Samaritans are not just children of Abraham, but are also descendants of Jacob i.e. children of Israel. However, they were seen by the "core" Jews as outsiders, almost like a half-breed between Jews and Gentiles because they had intermarried over the generations.

[15]"Ancestrally, Samaritans claim descent from the Israelite tribes of Ephraim and Manasseh (the two sons of Joseph) as well as from the priestly tribe of Levi, who have links to ancient Samaria from the period of their entry into the land of Canaan, while some suggest that it was from the beginning of the Babylonian Exile up to the Samaritan polity of Baba Rabba. Samaritans used to include a line of the tribe of Benjamin, but the line went extinct during the decline period of the Samaritan demographics. The split between them and their brothers, the children of Judah (the Jews),

---

[15] http://en.wikipedia.org/wiki/Samaritans

began during the time of Eli the priest, and the culmination was during the Kingdom of Israel and Kingdom of Judah when the Samaritans (then Kingdom of Israel) refused to accept Jerusalem as the elect, and remained on Mount Gerizim. The Samaritans say that Mount Gerizim was the original Holy Place of Israel from the time that Joshua conquered Israel.

"So, what was the major point of dissent between the Jews and the Samaritans? The major issue between Jews and Samaritans had always been the location of the chosen place to worship God; Jerusalem according to the Jewish faith or Mount Gerizim according to the Samaritan version.

"So when Jesus told the Samaritan woman, "It is time", the statement ran a lot deeper than conventional studies would illustrate. He said "the time shall come" which is a futuristic statement and if He had stopped there, those listening and reading would have forever waited for some event in the future without realising the event was/is relevant to them. So He didn't stop there, He added "And now is". If you think about it, He could have simply said the "time is now" but as with the first part of the statement where He would have lost those in the present at that time, so the second part is rendered so as to ensure that all those through time that read it understand that the present is the relevant period. The statement is an everlasting statement that has a beginning (and now is) but no end (the time is coming). His silence about the past may be inferred to mean that in the past, there was a relevance to the physical location of worship (and indeed the Bible alludes to that).

"Hold that thought for a minute.

"In other words, both groups (the Jews and the Samaritans) were holding on to a dogged truth that indeed was valid (even though not an absolute truth as Jesus pointed out) and each group simply refused to budge. It would seem as though they were in a rare deadlock where they were on opposing sides but both right. Or perhaps I should say a deadlock where neither was wrong or both were wrong – even I get confused depending on how you choose to look at it. The fact remains, **in terms of being right or wrong**, they were on the same side [both being right, or both wrong or both not wrong but not right] despite having very different views. Jesus acknowledged that the Samaritans undeniably worshipped, except that they were not fully aware of what indeed they worshipped but nonetheless, worshipped. He didn't fault their worship; he faulted their knowledge of the Being they worshipped. That in itself is extremely curious and I can't help pondering if that applies to most religious groups today – **worshipping without knowing what you worship and falling into various arguments with other groups when you all are probably equally ignorant of the Being you worship.**

"Jesus was, if you like, contradicting what both the Jews and the Samaritans had known and held for practically all of their existence. Jesus was deliberately and meticulously building a bridge to the Father, a bridge that was wider and more accommodating than what either the Jews or the Samaritans could have experienced or imagined.

Jesus' teachings were constantly focused on building a bridge as opposed to destroying what existed.

"To the Samaritan woman and indeed all who would listen, Jesus was saying that from now on, from this time till the end of time, forget what you did in the past, forget what you have ever known and have been taught, forget your traditions, forget your dogma, forget your inhibitions, forget your fears and forget your ignorance. Jesus first revealed the nature of the Father to the Samaritans (since He had told them they didn't know WHAT they worshipped). He said, "God is a Spirit". You cannot confine a Spirit to a geographical location and though it was accepted in the past, from this time forward, it is no longer necessary.

"In that one statement, in that single day, Jesus tore the fabric of dissent between the Jews and Samaritans and showed them that times and requirements had changed. However, evidently not all accepted what He said.

"The question is: did He make access to the Father more difficult or easier? Did He bring good news to those who were earnestly seeking the Father? Or bad news to those who wanted to monopolise Him? Did He make worship easier and more relevant? Did He take out the bottlenecks embedded in the worship they were familiar with? This is the true test of a change in a covenant especially where the intention is foreknown. Does the change make the intention easier or more difficult? Does the change liberate those who have struggled to achieve the purpose but were lost in tradition and dogma and doctrine? Does the change increase the number that will fulfill the intention or reduce it? If the answers are in the affirmative, why would you resist the change? Unless you intend to prevent more people from accessing the covenant!!!

"Who are the people we individually and collectively see as modern day Samaritans? Who are those that we exclude and condemn and refuse to have any alliance with because their method or means or place of worship is not the same as ours? Who are those that, in your extremely myopic opinion, do not know what they worship? But still they worship nonetheless. And of course, who are the modern day Jews? Or perhaps I should ask, who are the modern day Pharisees? Who are the people that sit in judgment of others simply because they are different? (or should I say because they sin different from them?) Who are the people who believe they have a superior understanding, whose minds are clouded by arrogance, who refuse to step down from their high horses yet claim ownership of and sole servitude to the Creator?

"The Samaritan woman is remembered a lot for her flaws (5 husbands) but a key quality is not often presented. A quality that I believe, if she hadn't exhibited, the conversation would not have progressed the way it did and redemption would have eluded her as it does many today. She said, "I know the Messiah is coming and when He does, He will declare all things to us." She made this statement **AFTER** Jesus had told her she didn't know what she worshipped. She could have taken offense in that alone, I certainly would have, but she didn't. Her statement showed a rare openness of mind, a willingness to accept whatever was the truth, an acceptance that that truth may not be what she has known – as long as she was sure that the truth came from the mind of God. It showed that she knew there were things she didn't know and it showed that she was willing to follow and obey the One who had the true message of God if and when she found Him. Only then did Jesus reveal Himself to her. My knowledge of the Bible is rusty, but I believe she was the first He revealed Himself to as the Messiah and probably the only in such direct terms.

"So, in summary, what happened to the Samaritan woman MUST happen to each and every human who truly intends to worship God – irrespective of religious inclination or denomination. It requires a rare humility that many would struggle to summon.

"Despite knowing what you are doing and having done it since forever, you must lay it all down and accept that there's a possibility of a better and easier way that can only come after the Father is revealed to you. You must also seek for that revelation and be willing to accept that what you know and what you oppose may both be wrong (or may both require changing).

"Here on earth, we see big buildings and daunting oceans. We are still exploring the Amazon. We have studied for hundreds of years and yet do not fully know our earth. Man is a small speck on earth while the earth is a smaller speck in the universe. I can assure you that, whatever your religion, no matter how many years you have been a worshipper of God, your knowledge of Him is infinitesimally small compared to who He really is.

"In seeking God, you will need to open your mind & heart and close your eyes & memory. Many people I know do it the other way round: Open their eyes and memory but shut out their minds and hearts."

OUR FOLLY

Pa Abraham went further, "over thousands of years, religion has become deeply rooted as part of the culture of mankind and not having one, or not professing to one, will certainly make you look like you don't believe in God or worse, that you probably worship the devil. Truth remains that it was mankind that invented religion to fill a void our mental capacity couldn't. When we, as mere mortals, try to understand concepts like eternity, creation, death, destiny, good and evil our minds go into overdrive and we invariably, hit a brick wall. Humans generally don't like this kind of brick wall. It reminds us that we are human and humans rarely accept not being able to conquer things. So, we conquer the brick wall by pretending to create a door – Religion. It's just a pretend door though, it doesn't really open, but we are satisfied that it's there and we make-believe that we can open it anytime we want. We often, however, get into differences about the size of the door, its colour, whether it swings in or out, or perhaps it slides and of course, how many can go through it and what type of people can. Those who all agree on the colour are in the same religion and those within the same religion who don't agree on whether it swings in or out, form a denomination. In all that, we quickly forget that the door was pretend in the first place and we stupidly start to fight each other over its attributes.

"That's the way we have decided to conquer the brick wall, if you can call that a conquest.

"Religion has become an unknown but acceptable variable that completes the parameters to an unknown equation. I'd be the first to admit that logically, that statement doesn't make any sense whatsoever, but we seem to prefer to have something that doesn't make sense, than to have nothing that doesn't make sense. It's just the way we humans are.

"God is a Spirit and I'm relatively certain that none of the circa 4,000 religious groups in the world today would dispute that. The worship of

God should and can only be done in spirit and in truth and He seeks such to worship Him.

"He has waited and waited for us to come to this point and accept the message that we have built a barrier to Him and not a bridge. It is time.

"Religion brings in and teaches us doctrine and procedure, it brings in the "laws of men" and sadly most often, binds us with self-inflicted chains and bonds, which the Almighty so desperately seeks to rid us of. Mankind seems to believe in working our way out of troubles and we apply this reasoning to the things of God and it ought not to be so. We seem to believe that the more we punish ourselves (or others) with whatsoever our religions dictate, then the more acceptable we are to God. We often find ourselves doing things our religion dictates and conforming to what is expected of people of our religion and we do this at the expense of what God demands and what He expects of us. We then subject His laws and desires for mankind to the scrutiny of religion and would only obey Him as long as His own laws conform to the expectations of our religion. I'd think that looking at it like that makes it rather insulting and obvious that, even with the right intentions, we miss the mark completely.

"Let's be sincere and honest with ourselves, "religion" as defined and practiced has only ever been a factor of division and not of bonding. It separates "us" from "them"; it separates the "accepted" from the "unbelievers"; it makes them, "infidels" and us "good".

"Where it ought to be used to bring unity and propagate brotherliness and peace, it seems its only use now is to exaggerate the slightest of tensions and cause pain, sorrow and bloodshed– it really should not be so. Even within a singular religious sect, you have dissent and splinter groups and denominations all because, we are trying to fit the Almighty God into our own personal small box, a really small box, that a religion dictates or worse, our own limited imagination. And when some people question the size of the box, or the rationale behind the parameters of the box, there is discord (some will even go as far as calling it blasphemy). At best, we get dissatisfied members or worse a war with a new denomination or even, a new religion.

"God wants the same thing for every human but sometimes He wants it in different ways from different individuals. In the corporate world we often speak about the folly in attempting to judge a monkey by how well it can swim or a fish by how well it climbs a tree. It is no different in the worship of God. He will ultimately judge us by the abilities He Himself has given us and we MUST not let other humans judge us by what they THINK we ought to be doing.

"If what I can do is pray and commune with my Creator every single hour, He will judge me if I do less simply because my religion dictates so. Or perhaps he has given me a voice and a manner of speaking that He finds pleasing to His own ears and my speaking to Him every hour is what He desires of me. But then, I become part of a religion that requires I pray in the morning and in the evening alone or perhaps only every other day and they convince me that that is all that is required of me. Or maybe I am great with playing musical instruments and I wish to use that talent to praise God and worship Him, but my religion oddly, doesn't agree that "noise" in the house of God pleases Him and I therefore ignore and quit the talent.

"God wants us to be with Him and to serve and worship Him. The only hindrance is SIN…. well that was until we had people bring in religion and start to worship that as well. Of course, in that instance, religion becomes a god and instead of worshipping the Father as you may think you are, you are actually engaged in idol worship – itself a sin. Your religion is your idol in such a case.

"Look within a religion like Christianity. There are "denominations" – some with such diverse beliefs that you wonder how they even co-exist under the same umbrella religious name and yet, they do. I would have guessed Christianity had 30-40 denominations, but when I did a check, I found that according to Gordon-Conwell Theological Seminary, there are roughly 43,000 Christian denominations worldwide as at 2012. I was truly dumbfounded, to say the least – 43,000!!!!!. But it buttresses my point. Now, imagine that each of these denominations broke out of Christianity and formed another religion based on the same beliefs that make up the differences in the denominations, we would have so many religions and yet, call on the same Almighty creator.

"It is of ultimate importance that we understand and at least attempt to see that the ways, thoughts and judgments of the Almighty have little if any to do with the sentiments or laws or expectations of mankind. This is an important concept, which if wholeheartedly accepted would cure mankind, at least those who claim to be religious, of most of the ills. It would focus us on the right path to worship. We would cease to be modern day Pharisees.

"I agree these may be considered conjectures, but they are certainly not entirely dismissible. What if someday, God gets frustrated with the fact that our many religions and doctrines are not fulfilling His one and only purpose of reconciling man to Himself? What if He sees that instead of pointing men AWAY from the one and only hindrance, SIN, we are instead pointing them and coercing them to religious groups, another hindrance? Would it therefore be out of place for Him to do something about it? Whether or not we like it, whether or not what He does is conventional, whether or not we choose to accept it, really won't make a difference to Him. He is NOT accountable to anyone, least of all, mankind – His own creation.

"He has told us in every conceivable way – using our conscience, our morals, through our folklore and even our fictional superhero stories; and as written in Holy Books in every religion, in every language, in every culture, by even the traditions we hold, "**Be reconciled to Him, serve only Him and eschew sin**". Frankly, it's hard to understand why such a simple request can be so hard to go about fulfilling.

"What He has done is to call each and every one of us as individuals, not any group whatsoever, but as distinct singular entities **NOT** into a religion, but to a **WAY of life**. A way of life HE has fashioned to give us peace and joy and fulfillment. "Follow me...I am the way" He said. I'm certain we all know, "Follow me" doesn't mean that we walk behind him wherever He goes and certainly doesn't mean find a Twitter handle called "The Almighty" and click follow. Neither does it mean follow a man who is a self-proclaimed follower of The Almighty or perhaps even a true follower; after all He didn't ask us to follow those that follow Him.

"We are called out of sin into a spiritual way of life where the law is simple and again, singular: LOVE - for God, self and mankind. God is a Spirit and to follow Him you CANNOT possibly walk in the flesh. You must walk and live as a spirit being with His guidance.

"Today we merely seem to try to call people out of one religion into another and in so doing, utterly miss the divine intent of the Almighty and thereby force Him to look for a way to make us understand His reconciliation intent and also create an easier way to illustrate His intent. It is of utmost importance to God to have a relationship with man for that is the entire and complete reason for our creation. He will pull all the strings, break all the barriers, and provide all that is required to create a way for us to head back to Him. Whether you belong to one religious sect or not, whether you speak a particular language or not, whatever it is, He wants mankind reconciled with Himself. I cannot possibly say it enough. There is one and only one obstacle to achieving that – SIN. Not religion. Not tribe. Not colour. Not language. But SIN.

"Jesus called Nicodemus, a Jew, not out of Judaism, but simply into a new lifestyle. Had Nicodemus been of any other religion, as we know them today, whether Hindu or Muslim or Christian, Jesus would have said the exact same words - you must be born again – that is, you must translate from being a physical being with a spirit to being a spiritual being with a body; you must learn [the] and live [by] the laws of the spirit, for no matter what religion you belong to, the Almighty is universally known to be Spirit and serving Him, walking with Him, communicating with Him, pleasing Him, is all distinctly a spiritual experience.

"I'd have to repeat this over and over and hope it eventually sinks: All through time, the Almighty has had one aim, a singularity of purpose which He has, in every language and tribe and dispensation made clear - "turn away from sin and serve me". Through the ages, through the history books, through Holy Books, He has consistently shown and been unequivocal that He hates sin. ALL His servants across every nation and tribe and tongue have been those who lived and made it a purpose to attain a pure life with Him devoid of sin.

"Whether He makes a way by penance, or alms, or praise, or sobriety, or forgiveness, or the death of animals, or He makes a way by the death of Christ - the multiplicity of methods He chooses is entirely His divine discretion, however, his purpose remains singular - cleanse mankind of sin so as to have a perfect reconciliation and relationship with us.

"Let's look at the Jews for a minute to understand God's intent: being a "JEW" is more than a mere religion - it is a way of life. It describes not just their method of worship, but their culture and judicial disposition. Jews are not of a singular geographical origin anymore - We have American Jews and Swiss Jews and Ethiopian Jews. Being a Jew lets you know the laws that are being followed and lets you know the cultural disposition with and the manner in which worship is done. In summary, it tells you of the complete WAY Of LIFE being adhered to.

"That type of structure sounds more like what God's intent is. God, our Almighty Father is concerned about our way of life. We have however, CONTRARY to his purpose, created religions and divided peoples and introduced strife and doctrines that have acted more as stumbling blocks than anything else. There is no longer a way of life embedded in the religions we have created. We merely profess a religion and more likely because it is what our parents introduced us to or brought us up to believe, we in turn believe that it is enough. It is not.

"I already spoke of Mahatma Gandhi and I'm sure we are aware of his famous quote: "I like your **Christ**, I do not like your **Christians**. Your **Christians** are so unlike your **Christ**."

"The word "Christian" came about sometime around AD 39-42 when Romans observed that a certain group of people behaved in a certain manner - sharing all things, loving each other, living in peace, caring for the poor and widowed, humbly serving each other, teaching eternity and spiritual edification, all which closely resembled the lifestyle of the Christ. These first "Christians", were a simple group made up of people of many nations and tribes and tongues and yes, also made up of many things we today call religions - but as a way of life, they were Christians.

"The Ethiopian Eunuch in the Bible is a perfect example of a soul sincerely seeking to worship the Almighty and was "born again" but was never asked or compelled to convert from whatever he was to something else. At least there is no such record and I doubt that there were other "Christians" in his home country when he got back. I have always wondered what happened and how he lived after his encounter with Philip. Did he start a church? I doubt it. Did his life change and perhaps others asked him what happened and perhaps many said they wanted to be like him – I certainly think so. I imagine him coming across today's type of Christian who would have probably judged him on sight and instead of noticing that his way of life and manners were quite similar to what God expects, would attempt to turn him to their religion. I can imagine what the Eunuch's reaction to that would be.

"I've also tried figuring out what religion Jesus would have fitted into. Jesus, just in case you haven't deduced it for yourself, was certainly not a Christian. He couldn't have been because the word "Christian" came into existence because of Him and long after He had left the earth. Now, we know the many stories of the clashes between Him and the Jewish scholars who accused Him of everything from heresy to blasphemy to being possessed with devils and though He may have been a Jew by birth, but the fact that the Jews killed Him for all the reasons they did, meant he wasn't quite accepted according to their ways.

"Again I cast my mind to Abraham who incidentally was also not a Jew, neither was Ishmael nor Isaac nor Jacob. These are the men who form the pillars of God's relationship and covenants with mankind. Throw in Adam and Noah and even Job if you please - the point remains, they all lived in a certain way, they had a way of life that pleased God. But curiously, they each had no religion.

"I also wondered why in the Bible God called Himself the God of Abraham, the God of Isaac and the God of Jacob and went no further. I still wonder and the main thing that comes to me is that after Jacob, came two things: religion and a nation. I may be wrong, but that's the only thing that pops out to me.

"I am not saying having a religion is a bad thing; I am saying that putting that religion ABOVE the way of life that the Almighty demands distracts you from truly worshipping and pleasing Him. If instead of doing what God wants you to, you tend to do what your **religion** dictates, worship when your **religion** dictates, be enemies of who your **religion** is enemy to, attempt to draw people from their **religion** to yours, then my dear friend, you worship your religion, not God. Doing that makes your religion, whatsoever you chose to call it, your god.

"Balaam, obviously not a Jew realised that the Israelites worshipped the same God that he did. He not only worshipped God, but Balaam was well known for his communication with God and the fact that God revealed things to him. I wonder what the modern day Christian would do should he come in contact with a Balaam. Would he hear him out? Would he reason with him to find out who his God is and see if perhaps He is one and the same as his? Or would he shut out all reason and only insist he be a lost soul unless he converts to some version of Christianity?

"In the New Testament, there's a record of a man called Cornelius, who certainly was a Gentile, but still, described as a [16]"devout, God-fearing man, who prayed continually to God" and obviously, God heard him. Was he praying to the same God the Jews of his time knew? An average Jew of that time would disagree because Cornelius was a Gentile. Even Peter who walked with and learnt from Jesus found it impossible, without God's personal intervention, to go to Cornelius. It then begs the question, how many people are outside your sphere of understanding of "children of God" but are, nonetheless children of God? How many would you imagine or condemn as lost simply because they are different from you; have a different understanding of God; or practice a different mode of worship; or have a different background?"

---

[16] Acts 10:1

CIRCUMCISION

"You certainly are circumcised, right? Have you ever wondered why? What the relevance is?"

"In all honesty, no I haven't wondered. It's just something we do, isn't it? And it has some positive health benefits."

"Circumcision was the mark of the covenant between God and Abraham. It was a specific mark of a specific covenant for a specific group of people to do a specific thing. To partake in that covenant, you had to be Abraham's seed and you then had to be circumcised. The whole Bible story is written to tell the story of how, why and for what purpose this covenant was made, then how the people that were party to the covenant reacted and behaved, how they disappointed the covenant, how God went out of His way to uphold it and then how His sacrifice was rejected by these covenanted people. The story continues with how God opened up a NEW COVENANT available to EVERYBODY since His plan and messenger were rejected by those who should have accepted it; those who it was designed for.

"So, this begs the question, is there a mark for partakers of this new covenant?

"Of course there is. It's exactly the same, but different.

"Remember the covenant with Abraham and his seed was a physical covenant for physical benefits for a physical amount of time. In line with drawing mankind closer to His nature, the new covenant is a spiritual covenant, for spiritual benefits for eternity (the spiritual non-measure of what we call time). Therefore, as you would expect, the mark of this covenant can't be physical. ***You still need to be circumcised, but it's a circumcision of your heart.***

"As a young boy is born and then some time later, he is circumcised, so it is with the spirit birth [remember what we discussed about being born [all over] again?]. Once you are born [all over] again as a spirit being, some time afterwards, when your spirit is ready, your heart is circumcised and just like the circumcision of the foreskin where the 'excess' is removed, so is the circumcision of the heart - the excesses are removed.

"First, the circumcision of the foreskin is painful; very painful and it's done to babies when they are born; but the pain wanes and then simply leaves just a mark. So is the circumcision of the heart done to [spiritual] babies when they are just born (again). The circumcision of the heart is also painful, very painful but the pain and struggles wane and then you are left with just a mark – the mark of a better being. If anyone tells you they do not know if their hearts have been circumcised, then chances are, they haven't. It's painful because the natural "skin" or "layer" of unwanted issues around the heart or mind are forcefully removed. All the things you would naturally want and desire and indulge in have to be forcefully removed until not wanting them becomes a habit. You have to willingly submit for this and the belief that it's automatic is false.

"If a Jewish family gave birth to a baby boy and refused to circumcise him, the boy would not die. He would live to a ripe full age but I guess he will not partake of the Abrahamic covenant.

"Same way, when you are born (again), if you do not circumcise your heart, you will not die – but when it's too late, you will realise that you cannot partake of the spiritual covenant available between you and God. You will exist but certainly not enjoy the spiritual existence because the covenant to keep you and prosper you as your soul prospers will not be yours. The covenant to bring you into eternal rest will not be yours.

"Circumcision of the heart is one of the laws of the spirit being that must be kept for your own good. Also, just as the physical circumcision helps you to keep physically healthy by keeping dirt and germs away, so is the spiritual circumcision by removing unnecessary desires. It helps to keep you spiritually healthy by keeping spiritual dirt and filth away from your heart.

"Just as you cannot circumcise an unborn child, the heart of an unborn (again) person cannot be circumcised.

"So, when you meet a Jew who is a partaker of Abraham's covenant, he proves it by showing you his...erm...how do I put it, foregone foreskin? (I wouldn't suggest you ask for that though. In today's world, you may be terribly misunderstood). The same way when you meet someone who claims to be partaker of the NEW covenant, it can be proven. (The covenant is better than Abraham's because it is everlasting - the spiritual unit for what we call time). He proves it by showing you (or himself at least) his heart. His heart is pure, well formed, devoid of worldly clutter, no extras hanging on – if his heart isn't so, then he isn't a partaker of the covenant. It's pretty simple."

There's absolutely no way I am not sticking close to this man. It's amazing how he just brings out the things I already know, but never gave a thought and simplifies them to a ridiculously practical level.

"Anyways, I still wonder how you knew I was the one that called the first time we spoke on the phone."

"Patience my son, in time."

"Also", he continued, "some people give the weak excuse that certain things, like certain bad habits are part of their nature; things they know aren't doing them good but they say, it's how they are or "that's how God made me." How many times have you heard that?"

I thought of quite a few of my friends and I wanted to answer, but very swiftly remembered the proverb about the number of fingers pointing back at you when you point at others. Common sense prevailed and I just smiled.

"Well, surprise surprise. God made all men with the foreskin but at some point He asked for it to be removed. How you are made, or how you have been, or what comes naturally to you is not a tenable excuse for indulging yourself in what is contrary to God's laws. Sometimes, you have to deliberately and painfully separate yourself from some of those habits or desires.

"Ponder on that!"

BENEFIT OF DOUBT

*"I once had the opportunity to meet a young lady who lost her mother to a horrible accident many years before and had recently also lost her father. Her father was a wealthy trader in a very large city. After her mother's death, her father had to sell all his goods and houses and took his daughter to live in a remote town with little civilisation. She had grown into a fine young woman and her father ensured she got the best of everything she **needed** including the best tutors. Her manners were impeccable and though she lived modestly, it was clear she lacked nothing. She told me that in her early years, she secretly despised her father in her heart and harbored a deep resentment for him because she knew he was wealthy and yet refused to move to the big cities where she would have had so much fun. Having endured such a remote lifestyle for so long, on her 21st birthday, she insisted on traveling to explore the world and her youth. Very reluctantly, her father agreed*

but with a single condition: that she read a letter he would write before sunset on the day she leaves.

"In the letter, he explained his extreme love for her mother and how he had to make a choice to save her life or his. Everyone in the city knew him as a truly great man, who was kind, generous and compassionate and there was never a time anyone who came to him in need left without being satisfied.

When he had to choose to let his wife die, the city became hostile and that was the reason he left. There was nowhere he went that the story of his horrible choice hadn't outrun him and so, he made a decision to sell all he had and to move where no one would have heard of him. He made that choice to protect his daughter from the venom of human nature. He made that choice to sacrifice all so that she could have a clean start. He made that choice because her mother was already dying of terminal cancer and had just days to live. Donating an organ would have made little difference. He made a choice not to, because she asked him not to. Had he not made that choice, his beloved daughter would have become an orphan in a matter of days, as he surely would've lost his life during the procedure.

"The world judged him and in its familiar cruelty, judged him wrong and without ever knowing the full story.

"There is a large group of people who are actively seeking the Almighty, who realise they are lost and who understand that there is more to life and living than merely existing. They look around, they observe those who claim to know and worship Him but they sense and often, even see the paradox. They contemplate all the religious bigotry, all the senseless bloodshed in the name of the Almighty, all the destruction justified by some as serving the Creator, the deceptions in the name of the Righteous One, the thieving in the name of the Benevolent. They therefore conclude that if this is His way and these are His servants, then they are better off on their own. Lives that would so willingly serve The Almighty are lost by the very ones who ought to be bringing them salvation. What do you think? On whom shall greater judgment fall? The sheep gone astray or the shepherd who slept while it happened? The child who walked through an open gate or he that left the gate open.

"Do not be deceived; one shall receive consequence and the other judgment. He who receives consequence may also receive mercy but he on whom judgment has been passed can only receive a long and painful sentence.

"We cannot see, we cannot perceive that we all call on the name of the same God, the Father of all, the Creator of the universe. We call on His many names in many languages and yet, we refuse to see. We divide each other, we kill each other, we judge each other and we all jointly flout the will of God in the name of serving Him. How can't we see?

"There's something we should be certain about and that is that the Almighty doesn't judge the same way we do. When we judge, we look to the things we know, perceive, think or attribute an action to. We are limited by our own knowledge and can err on so many counts. Our justice system is generally based on evidence that can be proved or evidence from witnesses which may or may not be biased. Perhaps, even outright lies.

"There are many things we experience that add up to the biases we hold:

1. Our individual upbringing and moral standards differ like day and night and this comes in to weigh on the judgments we make of circumstances and people.

2. Our expectations of others will be another major influencing detail regarding the judgments we come to accept.

3. Lastly, our instincts will play a major role especially when we have no observable fact or detail and absolutely no information to base a decision on. Yet, we come to a conclusion and say "our gut feel" led us to it.

"There are millions of people who will make a career choice, a life changing investment decision or reject a potential life partner based on something as inexplicable as a gut feel. Mankind certainly has many known fixed, even if not understood, parameters for making judgments and decisions.

"Seeing we know almost exactly how man makes his decisions and we know that [17]God doesn't base His judgments on the same parameters as man does, then it is safe to write a simple mathematical equation:

$$A \neq B \quad where \quad A = God's\ way\ of\ Judging\ and$$
$$B = Man's\ way\ of\ Judging$$

"Now, we can make an attempt to figure out A (which is like trying to remember a fact you have forgotten or to put it another way, "trying to know what you don't know").

---

[17] 1Samuel 16:7

"By exclusion though, we can limit or create a definition of a large SET which strictly excludes the parameters that make up B and therefore it is possible to have points we can use to deduce A. We may not know exactly what A is, but we would have a broad idea.

"We have the parameters of B (how man judges) and therefore know for a certainty, that those parameters are not relevant in defining A (how God judges) and it implies that everything that is known in B should not be part of A. So, God doesn't judge based on what we see, or what we know and all the factors we mentioned in the paragraphs above.

"The question now is, what are the things that man DOES NOT base his judgments on. For it is those things that would likely make up what God would base His on.

"So for example, please permit me to digress a bit here, if we met a man on our way to work and he was always either drunk or hung-over and I mean, every single time you met him and that would be a couple of times a week – how long before you either "talk to him" or start avoiding him? Most of us, if not all, will conclude, and by all measurable details, correctly too, that he had a terrible drinking problem. We may decide to associate much less with him and even ask potential suitors or friends to stay away from a man with that degree of irresponsibility.

"That's how man would judge. Imagine this man crossing the road, half drunk and run over by a car – we may even feel sorry for the car driver for the trauma such an irresponsible man, "who got what he deserved", caused.

"Now, imagine you make it to Paradise and you see this "ever-drunk" man right there sitting in the bosom of the Almighty. The angel on duty that day would see your bewildered face and probably ask you if you ever heard of [18]"Auto Brewery Syndrome"? I doubt that most people have ever heard of it. It's *a rare medical condition in which intoxicating quantities of alcohol are produced through endogenous fermentation within the digestive system.* In other words, your body converts carbohydrates to alcohol.

"There's indeed such a rare and extraordinary condition and the person may NEVER have had a taste of alcohol and yet is pretty much, perpetually drunk or hung-over.

---

[18] http://en.wikipedia.org/wiki/Auto-brewery_syndrome

"The Almighty who made him that way will certainly not see him the way we do nor judge him the way we do. It's not hard to see why ALL major religions have as their core teaching, "Love for your neighbour" (whether or not this core teaching is what is amplified is a totally different matter). You will not judge (or more accurately put, condemn) one that you love! And if you follow your religion's teachings and love all, then you will not fall into judgment for you will not be judging others. How can you even think of judging though, when there are so many things you perceive not?

"Back to our exclusion theory as the basis of the Almighty's judgment criteria. A pre existing and even possibly unknown and undetectable medical condition or hereditary disposition can affect a man's behaviour and therefore that fact would NOT form a basis for your judgment (because you are simply unaware of and cannot measure it) and it therefore means, it MAY be a criteria God would consider.

"Another example is DNA predisposition and hormone production or the lack of within the body. Mankind is still unraveling the mystery of DNA and we may understand the basics of how it affects things like height and weight and eye colour, but we know next to nothing about how it may possibly affect decision-making.

"So, we have a few parameters that are certainly outside the realm of possibility when man judges, mostly due to ignorance and a lack of grasp of phenomena outside our immediate understanding. We also have some idea around how man judges and so we can exclude that from the manner in which God judges. We also have some insight into how man doesn't judge and we can include that as a possible consideration of details God would entertain in His own judgment, especially as He created us and knows everything about us even better than we know ourselves.

"The point here, as is with all my lessons, is we cannot be anything but foolish if we try to play God. He is beyond all our vision and comprehension. The human mind is not created with the ability to grasp the entirety of His Being. Just as we cannot imagine a colour we have never seen, nor contemplate the state of timelessness so, we cannot even begin to comprehend the type of details He knows or the reasoning He has or the purpose He has devised, and yet, we are comfortable and feel justified in proclaiming, on His behalf, who His true worshipers are?

"We attempt to force others into our own way of thinking, into our own extremely limited knowledge of God's ways and believe that our tiny, minuscule, incomplete comprehension of a small aspect of a glimpse of the Almighty is a totality? Should anyone really feel justified in speaking in absolute terms on His behalf regarding things of the heart and mind and soul?

"We attack and diminish others and their faiths and their way of life because it doesn't conform to what we think we know? We refuse to see that in a much bigger picture we all are like the story of the 6 blind men trying to describe an elephant when each was observing and feeling a completely different part of it. And instead of putting all the knowledge together to get a complete, or at least, more complete picture, they all argued and quarreled that the other was wrong.

REUNION REALITY

Wow, I couldn't believe the excitement. I hadn't felt this way in ages. It had been many months since I last communicated with Pa Abraham.

It was like he fell off the planet or something. So when I randomly bumped into someone who also knew and had met Pa Abraham and even knew where he lived, I was beside myself in joy.

I drove to the address I was given and it was a bit surprising that the guard opened the gate once I mentioned I was looking for Pa Abe – for once, I had all the aces. I would surprise him beyond belief. I had pictured the look on his face with me standing at the front door. I couldn't contain myself, I couldn't wait to tell him how my life had changed and how I'd been able to impact a few others with nowhere near the difficulty I had even imagined. I couldn't wait to tell him that I was now truly born anew, had a fruitful relationship with God and yet, didn't feel like a typical churchgoer per se.

A young lady opened the door, extremely polite and to be honest, I hadn't seen a more beautiful woman in my whole life. It felt like the world paused as she opened that door; everything was in slow motion from then on. She was a unique blend of dark caramel colour with jet black all natural hair with a prominent streak of beautiful grey. She had hazel coloured eyes, full lips, subtly raised cheek bones, a dimple on the left side of her face and even with absolutely no makeup on, she was superbly stunning in the most delicate way.

"Good day ma'am, I'm here to see Pa Abe. He's not expecting me but I'd like to surprise him".

She smiled a soft, mocking smile and asked me to come in and sit. I could feel her stare very strongly and it was rather uncomfortable. I noticed she wasn't heading for the staircase where I imagined she would go to tell him he had a guest, but walking right behind me. As she sat, she asked why I wanted to see him.

I simply said he was my mentor, we lost touch and I found him again."When did he mentor you last?" she asked sinking even deeper into her seat, clearly with no intention of rising soon.

"A couple of months ago." My excitement made me a tad impatient.

She sat very upright and asked a series of very detailed questions about when I met him, what he told me of himself, of his life, of his family. She asked what he looked like, his age…where was this going, I wondered?

I spent the next 15 minutes trying, without success obviously, to rehash a 12 month relationship. I believe my unease was quite noticeable at this point. I was getting a little irritated and impatient. I think it was more apparent than I thought

She stood up rather abruptly, went to a large mahogany bookshelf, exactly what I had pictured when Pa Abe spoke about his vast book collection. There was a painting of an angel blowing a trumpet, which looked awfully familiar, and I was struggling to remember where I had previously seen it.

She literally threw the book at me – I smiled and tried to be as polite as I could.

"Did the book slip from you?"

She smiled back and said, "I see you have jokes, but I am not amused."

She asked if I had ever read the book.

"Nope, I haven't, why do you ask?"

Not surprisingly, she didn't answer. Her stunning beauty had started fading and she was suddenly looking more like the witch in Snow White.

"Pa Abraham was my grandfather, but he raised me himself after both my parents died in a car crash – oh, and by the way, the car crash you claim to have met him at describes the exact crash that killed my parents. He was everything you described and I wrote that book in memory of him."

Something always goes wrong when I try to surprise this enigma called Pa Abe. He somehow, always gets the better of me. Surely she must be mistaken.

"What do you mean in memory of him?"

"My grandfather passed away 5 years ago." Her face was straight, her back was straight, her gaze was straight...but why were her words crooked?

I laughed – it wasn't a laugh of amusement. There's this laugh when realisation slowly creeps into your nervous system, bypassing your brain and conscious function, and no, it doesn't tickle, but you laugh.

The room wasn't any hotter, but I could feel sweat running down my back. I stared deep into her eyes, looking for the "tell", waiting for her to burst out laughing for "having" me. I looked. I waited. She stared back – still quite unamused.

I turned her book over and there it was, Pa Abe's face. That peacefully stern face with a smile that leaves you with a calming feeling that's incomprehensible. Then it hit me. She wasn't teasing, she wasn't joking – but how do you handle two options that are both impossible? She wasn't joking, but the alternative wasn't possible.

It took a long time, at least it felt that way, before I could get any form of reasonable composure and I was able to convince her I wasn't playing a prank nor was I a lunatic.

We eventually sat, we ate, we talked, she shared memories, I held her hand. My eyes got cloudy first from the pain that I wouldn't see him again, then from the realisation that I probably never saw him in the first place. Tears rolled down my cheeks and then a soft sob and then I couldn't control myself as the floodgates were opened. I wasn't even sure if I was distressed that a man I knew, met and spoke with had died before I met him, or that I missed a friend – but how could he be a friend if I never met him? But I met him? After he died? All the thoughts in my head were really dizzying.

She seemed to realise what I was going through and she started to accept I wasn't delusional and the same emotions must have overwhelmed her as well because she too started sobbing. I think she then realised what had been happening.

Her voice became soft and comforting, albeit asking the most absurd of questions. "Are you sure you didn't meet him 5 years ago?"

Oh wow, perhaps I did meet him 5 years ago and then my brain went into a coma and the rest of my body functioned just fine. Or maybe I slipped and fell into a time warp or perhaps someone mistakenly clicked CTRL+ALT+DEL shift [select files] {years 27-32} of my life – I wasn't sure if I said the words or just thought them!

There's a prank somewhere. There's at least a major misunderstanding.

I showed her the prayer Pa Abraham had written for me and insisted I pray the words with sincerity every night for eight days till God answered me. I remember that I had asked him how I would know God had answered, and he told me not to worry, that I would certainly know. He gave only two conditions for saying the prayer:

that I say it with all sincerity of heart and that I share it with as many people as I can.

I pulled out the piece of paper with the prayer and asked her to have it – it was difficult leaving the only evidence of encountering Pa Abraham, but I was willing to.

Not entirely surprising though, I didn't have to: she had her own piece of paper with exactly the same prayer.

THE PRAYER

Creator of the Earth, Creator of the Universe, God of all Gods, the One and Only True God, the Almighty Father, The only One before whom I bow myself in worship

The only One I seek to follow and obey.

I wholly submit myself to your will and your divine ways.

I submit to your ordinances and your sovereignty.

I ask that you consider me, your creation.

I ask that you show me your ways that I may follow and abide in your statutes.

I ask that you judge my heart and my mind and my intentions.

I ask that I may be able to stand before you in purity of heart.

I ask that you accept me as your servant, as a Father accepts a lost son.

I ask that your ways and your laws may be written in my heart and that you reveal yourself to me that I may learn the way I ought to live, pray, serve you, worship you and honour you.

I vow to obey you and to reconcile myself and others to you and worship only you, The Creator of All, The One True God, The Everlasting Ruler of All.

I vow to abhor that which you have commanded that I despise – SIN.

I vow to love you and to show love to my neighbour with the same measure I show myself.

I ask that you give me the strength to love all and to seek to draw men to you.

Send your Holy Spirit to guide me, to direct me, to burn my hypocrisy and to teach me to truly serve you the way I ought, the way that pleases You.

I acknowledge that it is your will to reconcile me to Yourself.

I acknowledge that it is my sinful nature that makes approaching you so difficult and makes me hide behind many excuses to avoid facing you.

I acknowledge that you have sent so many prophets to warn and to guide me and you have caused them to write instructions in the Holy Books.

More than all these, you sent Jesus the greatest of all the prophets, the only one who lived without fault and the only one in whom you bestowed your Spirit without measure.

You are a Spirit and your Spirit is your DNA.

Jesus showed us how to live our lives in Love for You and ourselves and our fellow man.

He lived without fault and because He was such a Light to mankind, the Light created in the beginning, He was killed as the prophets said He would be.

I have never seen a man raised from the dead, but I look at the universe you created and I look upon the oceans and the animals living in them, I look upon the human body so complexly created in such harmony and I do not believe that, you who could make all these can be limited.

If I am required to merely believe that you raised Jesus from the dead, if you have made a way so simple as to only trust in you for what I do not understand, I shall.

I invite you into my life to teach me and show me how I ought to live that would please and honour you.

As I open my heart to you, I humbly await the manifestation of the quickening of my spirit being to be adopted into your family of True Worshippers.

Amen.

APPENDIX

In my quest for understanding my purpose in life, the Bible was able to give an extremely wide range of instruction encompassing virtually every sphere of life – from having a successful marital life, to principles for successful business endeavors, political suaveness and wisdom for instruction. Full understanding of the texts I came across formed key pillars for building the life I have today and that is why I bring this up with you.

In many instances, we are in too much of a hurry to read and move on to the next lesson that we lose the life-giving essence of the text we are merely skimming through and end up with only a partial understanding.

One passage that really struck me in the Bible is the one that mentions that "Jesus came to set the captives free" – I am sure you are familiar with that.

It sounds simple enough and many of the people I have interacted with can explain what it means. I haven't met many though, who can give the full extent of all the individuals covered by its meaning. There are so many that will read and not give the text a second thought because they believe that it doesn't apply to them – after all, they aren't "captives" or perhaps they aren't captives anymore.

This is probably because the most common interpretation I have come across for the text is in the context of captives meaning sinners and evil-doers, the bad of society and outcasts. Certainly, sinners are captives, but are they the only captives? I prefer to look at it from the point of view of understanding and identifying various masters and seeing which of these masters we serve willingly; for if our serving them isn't of complete free will, then we are captive to them. From that point of view, all of a sudden and outside of my narrow definition of sinners, a whole new world of captives emerged: Captives of family, habit, tradition, ignorance, fear, loyalty, mediocrity, career, ambition, failure, relationships, marriage, ancestry, past......the list is certainly no short one.

I would have loved to take you through each of them, but even if I did, we wouldn't exhaust the list. I was a captive of fear for so many years and I had a fear for the most awkward of things: success. I worked hard but just before each major opportunity for breakthrough, I'd get gripped with so much fear and terror that I'd blunder so badly and lose whatever edge I initially had. I saw it as bad luck, but it wasn't long before I realised that I was a captive of fear, the fear of success. It was extremely hard, absurd even, to accept that I feared success more than I feared failure – but that's what it was.

Of course, there are many couples that are trapped in and held captive by their marriages and they have absolutely nowhere to turn to and no way out.

In the studies of the person, Jesus in the Bible, He has shown, without a doubt, that indeed, whatsoever is holding you captive, His words, teachings and principles, if followed intently with sincerity of heart, will most certainly set you free. The Way he provides, leads you to freedom, and sanity, peace, joy, satisfaction and contentment.

Now, of all the groups of people that are held captive in various ways, there is one group that I feel the most empathy for because I believe they are the worst and most difficult set to free: The captives of RELIGION. These are people who preach and teach freedom to others while sitting in a tight prison and yet believe that they are free.

You can't set them free because they do not know they are held captive. They will laugh you to scorn at the mention of it.

In various cultures, you will find that the answers to the question "WHO is God?" wouldn't be too far different and they will reel out names showing His 'Almightiness" and "Supremacy". A common mistake you will come across is that many, perhaps most even, will give His attributes as His name as well. I have tried to explain that we need to understand and separate the names of God from His attributes. That He is Kind, Gracious, Merciful or a Provider are all attributes and yes you can say "God the Kind One" but that doesn't make Kindness His name. Why is this even important? The beginning of any relationship will generally start with a knowledge or exchange of names.

I am a man and yes, you may call me the sprightly one, but that doesn't make it my name, it's simply a description of me.

I don't believe that the human mind can fully grasp the Being we refer to as God. He lives, exists and operates under a completely different set of laws from what we can even imagine. Our knowledge of Him is so limited that even that is a mystery.

God never changes; but He doesn't stay the same!

Let me explain: water is liquid and if you freeze it, it changes and becomes solid. Now, if you heat it, it changes again and becomes steam. So, depending on some external conditions, water, as we know it, can change form. However, if you define water by its nature (H_2O) and not its attributes (liquid, solid or gas), then even though we observe changes, it stays the same. H_2O won't change in the examples above.

So what I mean is, God's nature NEVER changes but his attributes do. Too many know Him by His attributes and those attributes change depending on so many things: the individual, circumstance and dispensation; even His many names are really just naming His different and numerous attributes.

As it is impossible to ascribe a name of anyone and expect a reaction if the name is incorrect so also it is quite impossible for me to name The Father by any name other than that which He has revealed to us. Seeing we have very few names of God to go with, I came to a point where it became a lot more fruitful in understanding, not "WHO" but "WHAT" He is.

What is God? Yes we all believe he is a Spirit. But what is a Spirit? Isn't that the name given to an entity or some phenomenon we don't understand? Or is it our way of ensuring we have a collective and acceptable description of a Being we otherwise cannot describe? But yet again, is God just a Spirit?

I believe that by far, He must be a lot more than that.

BIOGRAPHY

The Author, Zeal Akaraiwe is on an exploratory journey to find the best ways to fulfill purpose on Earth. His blog, www.candleonahill.com, attempts to help people who sincerely desire to serve God to appreciate the simplicity of the Gospel.

Zeal hopes to spread light in a fast decaying world. He believes the responsibility for a better world and a better life lies with every human who has experienced God and not necessarily an exclusive group of preachers or evangelists.

Printed in the United States
By Bookmasters